Feasts Afloat

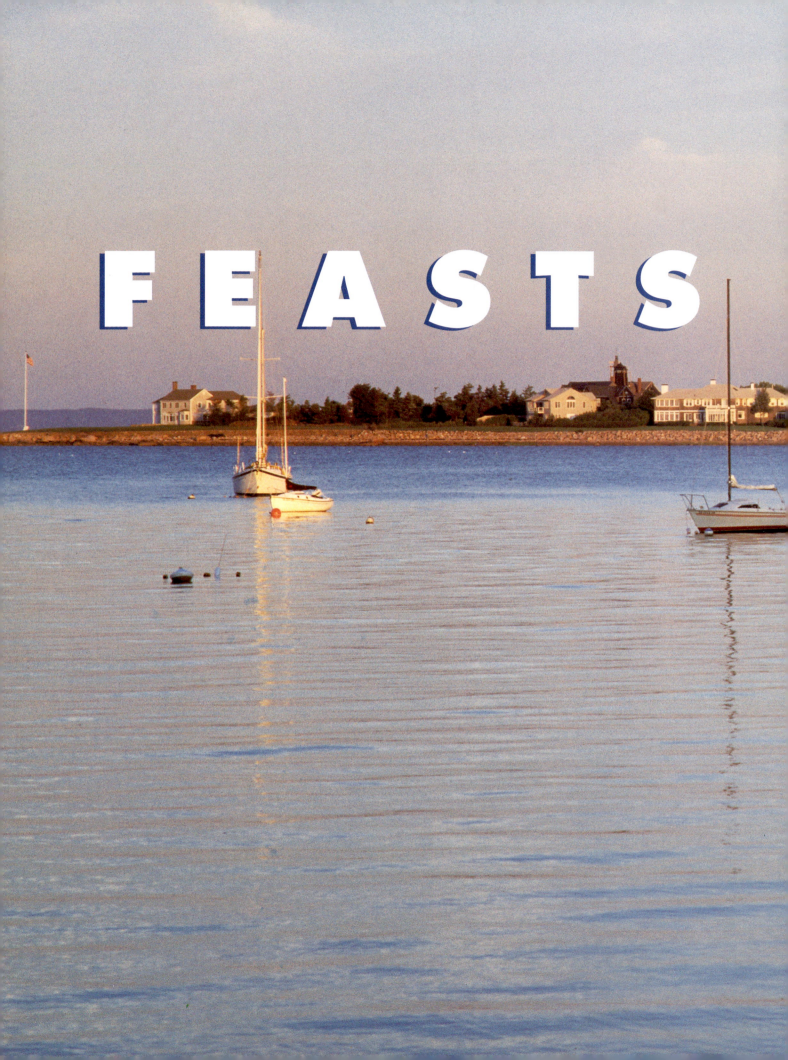

FEASTS

Jennifer Trainer Thompson
and
Elizabeth Wheeler

AFLOAT

150 Recipes for
Great Meals
from Small Spaces

Photographs by
Kristen Brochmann

Ten Speed Press
Berkeley Toronto

Ten Speed Press
Box 7123
Berkeley, California 94707
www.tenspeed.com

Distributed in Australia by Simon & Schuster Australia, in Canada by
Ten Speed Press Canada, in New Zealand by Southern Publishers Group,
in South Africa by Real Books, in Southeast Asia by Berkeley Books, and in
the United Kingdom and Europe by Airlift Book Company.

Book design by Ken Sansone

Grateful acknowledgment is given for use of the following: on pages
21 and 153, from *The Cook Is the Captain* by Neil Hollander and Harald
Mertes, John Murray (Publishers) Ltd.; on page 24, *Nautical Quarterly,*
Spring 1986; on page 49, from the 1965 edition of *A Cruising Guide to
the New England Coast* by Roger F. Duncan and John P. Ware. Copyright
© 1965 by Dodd, Mead & Company. Reprinted by permission of the
Putnam Publishing Group; on page 85, Copyright © 1942 James Thurber.
Copyright © 1970 Helen Thurber and Rosemary A. Thurber. From
"The Story of Sailing" in *My World—and Welcome to It,* published by
Harcourt Brace Jovanovich, Inc.; on page 112, from *The Cruising Lifestyle*
by John Rousmaniere; on page 119, copyright © 1985, 1988 by
John Rousmaniere; on page 154, "Be Prepared" Girl Scout motto.

Photographs on pages 114–115 copyright © 1990 by Doug Carver

Library of Congress Cataloging-in-Publication Data on file with the
publisher.

This material originally appeared in *The Yachting Cookbook* by Elizabeth
Wheeler and Jennifer Trainer, copyright © 1990 by Elizabeth Wheeler and
Jennifer Trainer, photographs copyright © 1990 by Kristen Brochmann,
published by Crown Publishers, Inc., New York.

Printed in Hong Kong
First printing, 2000

2 3 4 5 6 — 05 04 03 02 01

Acknowledgments

There are many people we would like to thank for their generous assistance while we wrote this book:

To Andy Anderson, Mary Barnard, the Brewster family, John and Kay Clark, Jay Connolly, Peter Duble, Sr., Dr. Davis Gallison, Edwin Gaynor, Fritz and Bronson Hager, Russell Hiller, Walter Krasniewicz, Nick LaForgia, Lars Malmborg, Bruce Marek, John and Marjorie Pannell, Emmy Peterson, the Price family, Sally Purcell, Laars Rudd, John Robertson, Carl Sherman, Riggs and Nan Smith, Bob and Barbara Tiedemann, and Robert van Ost for graciously loaning us their wonderful boats, beaches, and islands.

To Brandt Aymar, Lisa Ekus, Stuart Krichevsky, and Ken Sansone for their good will and interest in our work.

To Chris Duble, Nancy Duble, Colleen Heslip, Michael Newberry, Pam Parziale, Sarah Purcell, and Kent Rush for their dedicated tasting and testing, with a special thanks to Sarah for her help in creating a delightful dock party in the Thousand Islands.

To Ruth Keith, Phyllis McDowell, and Joan Wyer for their gracious hospitality.

To Matthew Benson, Julian Bond, Jeff Burnett, Bill Burnham, John Burnham, Marc Carmichael, Peggy Couch, Roswell and Angela Curtis, Peter Davis, Eliza Gaynor, Chris Harley, Missy Harvey, Glenn Little, John Macmillan, Dan Merritt, Jocelyn Moreland, Bill Morrissey, Don Porter, Paul Rathé, Beth Russell, Erik Soper, Jeannine Soper, and Mitzi Wheeler for their generous assistance and expertise.

To Madge Morris, Janet Woods, and the staff at the St. Vincent and the Grenadines Tourist Office; Tony Sardine and the staff at the Grand View Beach Hotel on St. Vincent; Yvone Cato, Snakey, and the staff at the Cotton House on Mustique; Basil Charles and Patrick Gibson at Basil's Bar on Mustique; and American Airlines and LIAT for paving the way.

To Karl Heinz Pfitzenreiter of J. A. Henckels, Scott Van Hensbergen of the Green River Trading Company, and our friends at The Complete Kitchen in Darien, Connecticut, for providing us with invaluable equipment. Also, to Brian Alden, Buzzards Bay Sailboards, Chicama Vineyards, Cointreau America, Crosswoods Vineyards, Cuisinart, Dry Creek Vineyards, Faïence, Festivities, Harbor Wines, Japan Oxygen, Joy-o-Loons, Magma Products, Majestic Gifts, The Outlet, The Place in Darien, Rolling Hills Farm, Sippican Wine Company, S. Pellegrino, Trappist Preserves, Twin Bird U.S.A., Vuarnet, Waldenkids, West County Cider, Williamsport Antiques, and Williams-Sonoma for their generous assistance.

To David Gonzales, Mary Goodbody, Dorothy McGhee, Kathy Norwood, and Tim Weyland for their valuable critiques.

To Doug Carver and Weston Andrews for their beautiful photographs of our early sailing days.

To Hugo Churchill (el guapo), who saved us from computer disaster countless times.

To Scott Wheeler for his support, helpful comments, and expert wine recommendations.

To Ellie and Potter Trainer and Peter Duble, Jr., for their unflagging support and enthusiasm.

This book is dedicated to Peter Wright Duble, Jr., whose wholehearted enthusiasm for life was obvious in everything he did—and who took more pleasure in eating grilled leg of lamb on a classic 12-meter than anyone we know.

Contents

ENTERTAINING ABOARD

INFORMAL FARE

Introduction

Our friendship began one sunny day in October nine years ago when we were hired to help deliver a forty-foot sloop from Mount Desert Island, Maine, to the British Virgin Islands. Elizabeth was the cook, and I was the second mate. Elizabeth had already gained a reputation in the Caribbean as a talented boat chef, and the delivery captain went to great lengths to find her for this twelve hundred-mile passage.

Working in cramped quarters on tempestuous seas, Elizabeth produced extraordinary meals that would have amazed people on land, let alone on a small boat in the middle of the ocean. We had crêpes and omelets for breakfast, cold soups for lunch, and freshly caught fish for dinner. When the captain sighted land after fourteen days at sea, Elizabeth disappeared below for a half-hour, then passed up freshly baked scones in honor of the occasion.

On an ocean passage one draws richness from simple things—watching the sun rise, pouring a bucket of seawater over your body in the tropical heat, sipping strong coffee topside on a starry night. Elizabeth's meals became a focal point of our daily life, enhancing the esprit de corps that comes from living with others on a boat.

By the time we landed in Virgin Gorda our friendship had been cemented by the many special meals and experiences we had shared. The afternoon of our arrival, after charging down the dock in search of ice cream and freshwater showers, the entire crew pitched in to create an inspired farewell dinner amid the palm trees and sapphire waters of our tropical anchorage. It was during this celebration, as we toasted our successful passage through the North Atlantic, that Elizabeth and I first entertained the notion of writing a cookbook.

Alas, it was not to be—at least not then. After several boat deliveries we went our separate ways. Elizabeth spent one final season cooking on charter boats, then moved to Connecticut, where she pursued a cooking career that included catering, teaching, and writing about food. I moved to Manhattan and, after a brief stint in the publishing industry, pursued a writing career. Along the way I moved to the Berkshire mountains of Massachusetts and got involved in the food world when my husband became a grower of shiitake mushrooms.

Through the years we kept in touch. In the fall of 1985, while working together to promote shiitake mushrooms at a food conference in Philadelphia, Elizabeth and I reminisced about our sailing days together—grilling halibut off the stern in Pulpit Harbor, sipping piña coladas in Cane Garden Bay, diving for lobsters in the Bahamas. We even laughed about the night we went aground on Duxbury Beach, and the clam chowder we devoured. Slowly, in that crowded conference booth—as the aroma of Elizabeth's grilled shiitakes drew food lovers like bees to honey—the idea of a yachting cookbook was reborn.

We approached the book with the belief that good food need not be difficult to make. If nothing else, we hope that *Feasts Afloat* demonstrates that one can easily create a gracious meal with a minimum of fuss: You don't need all the time, ingredients, and equipment typically associated with an imaginative dish. With the exception of those intended to be prepared ashore, the majority of dishes can be made with minimal cooking equipment. Although we have had the pleasure of cooking on large, luxurious yachts, we gained much of our experience by slugging it out in galleys with two burners, a cooler, and buckets of sea water.

We also believe that you needn't own a boat to use this book. Basically, *Feasts Afloat* explains how to make the best food under the worst conditions. We have found these recipes useful in a mountain cabin with no electricity, in a ski house in Vermont, and in several cramped New York City apartments. Indeed, on a stifling August afternoon in lower Manhattan, we've whipped up frothy strawberry daiquiris, closed our eyes, and imagined ourselves back on sybaritic St. Barts. Likewise, on crisp October nights in the Berkshires, the hearty minestrone is as comforting as it ever was on a foggy evening in Maine.

After logging 25,000 sea miles, we realize that—next to a well-developed sense of humor—the best attribute a sea cook can cultivate is flexibility to respond to the challenge of cooking in a minimal galley in remote places. For that reason, we have included variations at the end of recipes to allow for substitutions, and also to encourage the cook to consider these recipes as a point of departure.

Throughout our lives some of our most vivid memories have been of times when we were sailing. We love the exhilarating experience of guiding a boat over a seemingly limitless ocean and the sheer joy of being outdoors. Similarly, food prepared simply and shared with friends is one of our most basic and satisfying pleasures. To combine the two—at a lovely anchorage or on a vast ocean—is sublime.

JENNIFER TRAINER THOMPSON

DINNERS AFLOAT

Grilling on the Rail

PRECEDING PAGES: Savoring the early evening light is a great pleasure.

Mere mention of the word *grilling* conjures up rich memories of summer outdoor gatherings and the intoxicating aromas of food cooking over charcoal. To this day, grilling remains our favorite way to cook dinner.

Grilling is also an easy, informal way to entertain. We love to sit with friends in the cockpit at sunset, talking over drinks and hors d'oeuvres, while dinner sizzles on the grill. On the smallest boat, the possibilities of shipboard cooking are expanded enormously with a portable grill. (We've even been known to tote a hibachi along on springtime white-water canoe trips in northern New England.)

One of the best aspects of grilling is the easy cleanup: There are no pans to wash after dinner. Simply allow the ash to cool overnight and tip it into a trash bag in the morning. We recommend using a stainless steel grill that clamps onto the stern rail or is otherwise mounted to hang over the water. This prevents ash and embers from burning the deck. Look for a portable model with an attached lid that is easily assembled and can be taken ashore for beach cookouts.

The following menu is inspired by the Caribbean, where grilling is a way of life on boats. Drawing on native pork as well as locally grown fruits and vegetables, this casual meal is cooked almost entirely on the grill.

Grilled Lime-Marinated Pork

SERVES 4
PREPARATION: 10 minutes
COOKING: 20 minutes

Citrus juice is a natural tenderizer. The small, thin-skinned limes found in abundance in the Caribbean provide pork with a fresh zing, but grapefruit juice can be substituted.

4 boneless pork cutlets, pork chops, or meaty country-style pork ribs (about 1 inch thick)
Juice of 2 limes (about 3 tablespoons)
4 tablespoons vegetable oil or olive oil
2 teaspoons cumin seed, crushed
1 teaspoon dried oregano
2 garlic cloves, crushed
2 fresh chiles, chopped, or 1 teaspoon crushed red pepper
Freshly ground pepper
½ teaspoon salt

■ Place the pork in a shallow nonmetallic dish or heavy plastic bag. Combine the remaining ingredients and pour over the pork. Turn the meat in the marinade to coat thoroughly and let stand in a cool place 1 to 3 hours.

■ Prepare the grill (page 13).

■ Place the chops on the grill and sear them on both sides. Cook approximately 8 minutes per side, moving chops to a cooler spot on the grill if they brown too quickly.

Note: Country-style pork ribs should be cooked over a slow fire for approximately 30 minutes.

Suggested Wine: Beaujolais or a light-bodied Zinfandel.

Fresh Hot-Pepper Sauce

MAKES 1½ cups
PREPARATION: 15 minutes
COOKING: 10 minutes

The pepper sauce found along with salt shakers on the tables of island restaurants is *the* Caribbean seasoning. The peppers —or chiles—most commonly used are the tiny, pointed bird peppers, the crumpled-looking Scotch bonnet, or the long, scarlet cayenne. Each island has several varieties of hot sauce ranging from thick, seed-flecked pastes to the brilliant red "pepper wines." Searingly hot, they should be approached with caution. This homemade sauce is excellent with grilled meats, chicken, and fish.

1 large onion, grated or finely chopped
¼ cup freshly squeezed lime juice (about 4 limes)
1 cup water
2 garlic cloves, finely chopped or pressed
1 tablespoon finely chopped fresh chiles, or more to taste
½ teaspoon dried oregano
½ teaspoon salt
1 or 2 fresh tomatoes, seeded and finely chopped (optional)
¼ cup olive oil

■ Mix the onion and lime juice in a small nonmetallic saucepan and let stand at least 1 hour. Add the remaining ingredients and bring to a boil over moderate heat, stirring occasionally. Remove from heat and cool.

Grilled Eggplant

SERVES 4
PREPARATION: 30 minutes
COOKING: 20 minutes

In the open markets of the Windward Islands women sell a variety of home-grown vegetables including small, chubby purple eggplants that are tender, sweet, and ideal for grilling.

4 small eggplants (about ½ pound each)
Salt
Olive oil

■ Prepare the grill (page 13).

■ Cut each eggplant in half lengthwise, leaving the stems attached. Score the cut surface of each half in a diamond pattern about 1 inch wide and ½ inch deep. Sprinkle the scored surfaces with salt and turn the pieces face down to drain for about 20 minutes. Rinse eggplant quickly and squeeze gently to remove excess moisture.

■ Brush the eggplant halves lightly with oil and place them cut side down on the grill. Cook slowly, taking care not to brown the eggplant too quickly, for about 10 minutes. Turn the eggplant skin side down and cook until tender, about 10 minutes.

Smoky Eggplant Dip: A delicious dip can be made from grilled eggplant. When the grilled eggplant is cool enough to handle, scoop the flesh into a bowl, discarding the skin. Using a fork, mash the eggplant to the consistency of a coarse puree. Work in lime juice, wine vinegar, or a few chopped capers and enough olive oil until the mixture is thick and saucelike. Add chopped garlic or onion and chopped fresh parsley or celery leaves, and season to taste with salt. Serve with celery cut into short lengths, sliced French bread, or crackers.

GRILLING TIPS
■

Keep the grill surface clean and oiled to prevent food from sticking. (Spraying the grill with a nonstick vegetable spray before cooking also makes cleanup easier.)

· Brush food lightly with oil before putting it on the grill.

· Soak bamboo skewers in water for an hour before using to prevent them from catching fire.

· A grill cover helps food cook faster, keeps meats juicier, and conserves fuel.

· After a gas grill has been used several times, the lava rocks become greasy from fat and marinade. Turn them occasionally to burn off the fat.

· Never leave a grill unattended, especially in harbors, where the wake from other boats can send your dinner overboard or marauding seagulls can swoop down and make off with your pork chops.

· Before grilling at a slip, note the wind direction. You don't want to blow ash and smoke onto your boat or those nearby.

Marinated pork chops, eggplant, and cabbages ready for grilling.

Grilled Cabbage

SERVES 4 to 6
PREPARATION: 10 minutues
COOKING: 15 minutes

The loose-headed cabbage grown in the Windward Islands, usually no bigger than a grapefruit, is easy to store on a boat.

*2 to 3 small heads cabbage (about
    1 pound each)*
Olive oil
Salt
Vinegar

■ Prepare the grill (page 13).

■ Remove and discard any wilted or bruised outer leaves from the cabbages. Trim the stems flush with the base. Cut each cabbage in half lengthwise, keeping the leaves attached to the core. Steam cabbages or boil them in salted water about 1 minute, or until they are slightly wilted and their color brightens. Drain and set aside to cool. When the cabbage halves are cool enough to handle, gently squeeze to remove the excess moisture.

■ Brush the cut side of each cabbage half with olive oil and place cut side down on the grill. Cook about 10 minutes, checking so that they do not burn. Brush the cabbages lightly with more oil, turn, and cook for 10 minutes longer, or until lightly browned. Cut each piece in half if desired and sprinkle lightly with salt and a few drops of vinegar. Serve hot or at room temperature.

Grilled Pumpkin

SERVES 4 to 6
PREPARATION: 10 minutes
COOKING: 15–20 minutes

The hard-shelled green pumpkins found in most Caribbean markets have firm, yellow-orange flesh that tastes like butternut or Hubbard squash. Grilling lends a delicious smoky flavor to the pumpkin and requires little preparation.

*2- to 3-pound piece of pumpkin, skin on,
    cut into ¾-inch slices*
Olive oil
Salt

■ Prepare the grill (page 13).

■ Brush the pumpkin slices with olive oil and place on the grill. Cook about 15 minutes, or until the pumpkin can be pierced with the tip of a sharp knife. Remove the pumpkin from the grill and salt lightly before serving.

Variation: To bake pumpkin, season the slices with salt and pepper, and dot with butter and brown sugar. Wrap tightly in foil and cook on the grill until tender, about 45 minutes.

Corn Salad with Walnuts

SERVES 4 to 6
PREPARATION: 15 minutes

This creamy salad is a good addition to a grilling menu.

*1 16-ounce can water-packed corn
    kernels, drained*
*1 green bell pepper, cored, seeded, and
    chopped*
2 to 3 scallions, sliced fine in rounds
*3 tablespoons freshly squeezed lime or
    lemon juice*
2 teaspoons sugar
1 cup sour cream
4 tablespoons vegetable oil
Salt
Tabasco (optional)

Garnish
Tomato wedges
½ cup coarsely chopped walnuts

■ Place the corn, bell pepper, and scallions in a mixing bowl. Mix in the lime juice, sugar, sour cream, and oil. Add salt to taste and a few drops Fresh Hot-Pepper Sauce.

■ Serve cold, garnished with tomato wedges and walnuts.

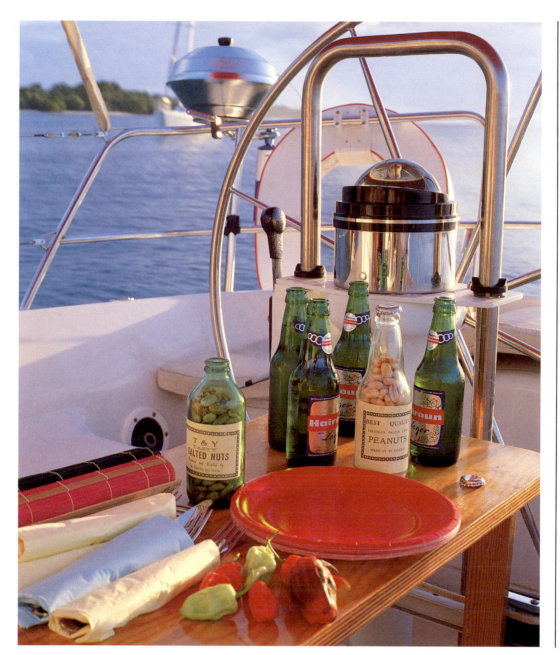

While in the Grenadines, we favor local beer and island-grown peanuts for the cocktail hour.

BELOW LEFT: Portable gas-fired grills are convenient for cruising. **B**ELOW RIGHT: Sugar-crusted grilled pine-apple.

What kind of grill should you use on a boat: gas or charcoal? Although many food enthusiasts prefer the rich, smoky flavors yielded by a charcoal grill, we've used both to good effect. Some notes:

Gas grills are easy to operate and won't smudge the decks with greasy ash. Although grill fittings and gas are readily available in the United States, they can be hard to find in remote parts of the world. When cooking with gas, always grill in open or well-ventilated areas. Otherwise, leaking gas could accumulate in the bilge, be ignited by a spark, and explode. Check the connections between the gas bottle and grill by brushing them with soapy water. If small bubbles form, shut off the gas and tighten the connection.

Although *charcoal grills* can be messy, briquets are available worldwide. (If you find yourself in remote parts of the Pacific without charcoal, however, use old coconut husks. They take longer to ignite but smolder wonderfully.) Before building a fire, line the bottom of the grill with foil to prolong the grill's life and make cleanup easier. The secret of successful grilling is even, powerful heat from fully ignited coals. Therefore, although the temptation may be great, refrain from cooking until the coals are covered with a light gray ash, about 30 to 40 minutes.

Radish and Cucumber Salad with Yogurt

(ALTERNATE RECIPE)

SERVES 4 to 6
PREPARATION: 15 minutues

A cool, crunchy salad, perfect for a hot summer night.

3 medium cucumbers, peeled, halved, and seeded
6 large radishes
1 garlic clove, finely chopped
3 to 4 tablespoons chopped fresh parsley or mint
2 tablespoons olive oil
1½ cups plain yogurt
Salt
Lemon juice or vinegar
½ cup chopped walnuts

■ Cut the cucumber halves crosswise into ¼-inch slices and place them in a large bowl. Slice the radishes into thin rounds, and add them to the cucumbers.

■ Add the garlic and parsley and toss. Stir the oil into the yogurt and mix until thinned and smooth. Add the yogurt mixture to the vegetables and stir well.

■ Season to taste with salt and lemon juice, and sprinkle with chopped walnuts.

Note: Once cut, cucumbers exude moisture, so serve this salad within a few hours.

Grilled Pineapple

SERVES 4 to 6
PREPARATION: 15 minutes
COOKING: 10 minutes

1 large ripe pineapple
6 tablespoons (¾ stick) unsalted butter, melted
1 cup brown sugar

■ Prepare the grill (page 13) and adjust the heat to low.

■ To remove the pineapple's leafy crown, grasp it firmly in one hand while holding the fruit with the other, and twist it off with a swift wrenching motion.

■ Using a sharp knife, cut the pineapple crosswise into 1-inch-thick slices. Neatly cut away the green rind from each slice. (Or, if you prefer, after removing the leaves cut a thin slice from the base of the pineapple so that it stands upright. Slice off the prickly rind, cutting deep enough to remove most of the eyes. Remove the remainder of the eyes with the tip of a paring knife. Then cut the pineapple crosswise into 1-inch-thick slices.)

■ Cut each pineapple slice into 4 wedges and trim off the hard core.

■ Brush the pineapple slices lightly with melted butter and place in a dish of brown sugar. Turn to coat the pieces on both sides and set aside for 15 minutes. Grill 2 to 3 minutes on each side until lightly browned.

Dinner on the Mooring

From the balcony of Elizabeth's house in Connecticut we can watch the boating ritual that takes place in Wilson Cove during the summertime. On Friday night boat owners arrive, hauling their gear and groceries down to the dock. They spend a few hours stowing, tinkering, and gossiping with neighbors. Early Saturday morning they return and are soon heading out to Long Island Sound for a weekend cruise. They motor back into the cove late Sunday afternoon, looking sunburned and satisfied.

With just one night on the boat, people naturally want to enjoy a special dinner. Although complex, multicourse meals are impractical, with a little advance planning one can easily produce an elegant meal from a small galley. The following dinner starts with spiced nuts and cut raw vegetables, which can be prepared on Thursday night. The lamb can also be marinated as many as two days in advance. The ingredients for the tomato salad can be packed ashore for assembly aboard, while the dough for the cookies can be made and frozen a week in advance, then baked several days ahead and stored in an airtight container. The ripe peaches only need to be wrapped carefully to prevent bruising.

Tomato Salad with Feta Cheese and Olives

SERVES 4 to 6
PREPARATION: 15 minutes

The success of this bright summer salad depends on the quality of the ingredients—use only the ripest red tomatoes and an excellent fruity olive oil. Serve with toasted triangles of pita bread or crusty bread to sop the delicious juices.

> *4 or 5 ripe firm tomatoes*
> *6 ounces crumbled feta cheese,*
>   *approximately*
> *Fresh parsley, dill, basil, or mint*
> *Olive oil*
> *Vinegar*
> *Olives*

■ Cut the tomatoes into wedges or thick slices and arrange on a platter or individual plates. Scatter the feta over the tomatoes, or pile in the center of the tomatoes. Tear the herbs and scatter over the tomatoes and cheese.

■ Drizzle olive oil over the salad and sprinkle with a few drops of vinegar, or serve with cruets of oil and vinegar. Decorate each plate with herbs and a few olives.

MENU

Spiced Almonds
(page 57)

Raw Vegetables

Tomato Salad with
Feta Cheese and
Olives

Grilled Butterflied
Lamb with Mustard
Vinaigrette

Roasted Summer
Vegetables

Pecan Moons

Peaches

■

DINNERS AFLOAT

OPPOSITE TOP: Grilled butterflied lamb sliced for serving. **O**PPOSITE BOTTOM: Marinated summer vegetables ready for roasting.

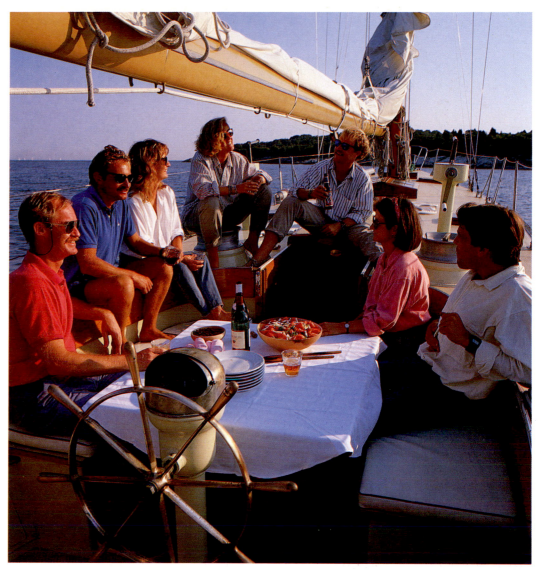

RIGHT: Enjoying the sunset after sailing off Newport on *Northern Light,* a 1938 wooden 12-meter.

RIGHT: This tomato salad is a refreshing first course.

Grilled Butterflied Lamb with Mustard Vinaigrette

SERVES 4 to 6
PREPARATION: 10 minutes plus 1 hour marinating
COOKING: 30 minutes

Our friends are crazy about this dish.

1 6- to 7-pound leg of lamb, boned and butterflied
3 garlic cloves, crushed
2 teaspoons crumbled dried rosemary
4 tablespoons Dijon mustard
Freshly ground pepper (or substitute 1 tablespoon crushed green peppercorns in brine)
3 tablespoons freshly squeezed lemon juice (about 1 lemon)
2 tablespoons dry sherry, Madeira, or vermouth
2 tablespoons soy sauce
4 tablespoons olive oil or vegetable oil

■ Trim excess fat from the surface of the lamb.

■ Rub the lamb with garlic, rosemary, mustard, and a generous amount of pepper. Place the lamb in a heavy plastic bag with the remaining ingredients. Expel the air from the bag and close the opening tightly. Distribute the marinade by moving the meat around in the bag. Marinate the lamb, turning it occasionally, for 1 to 3 hours at room temperature. Or refrigerate the lamb up to 2 days, and allow it to come to room temperature before cooking.

■ Prepare the grill (page 13).

■ Cook the lamb on the grill about 15 minutes per side for medium-rare lamb.

■ Remove the lamb to a carving board, cover, and allow to rest 10 minutes before carving. Serve with a spoonful of Mustard Vinaigrette (recipe follows) or Green Sauce (page 97).

Suggested Wine: A California Merlot or a red Bordeaux such as St. E'milion or Pomerol.

Mustard Vinaigrette

2 tablespoons Dijon mustard
1 to 2 tablespoons finely chopped shallots or onion
1 garlic clove, finely chopped
¼ cup freshly squeezed lemon juice (about 2 small lemons)
Salt
¾ cup olive oil or vegetable oil
2 to 3 tablespoons finely chopped fresh mint, or 1 tablespoon dried mint

■ Combine the mustard, shallots, garlic, lemon juice, and salt in a bowl, and blend with a whisk. Whisk in the oil gradually to make a creamy emulsified sauce.

■ Stir in the mint and taste for seasoning.

SMOKE SIGNALS

■

Give food a delicious smoky flavor with hardwood chips such as apple, hickory, mesquite, or oak. Soak a handful of chips in water for 10 minutes and toss them onto lava rocks or charcoal just before putting food on the grill. The chips will smolder rather than burn, smoking the food and sending out an incredible aroma that will tempt neighboring yachtsmen to row over and see what's for dinner.

Roasted Summer Vegetables

SERVES 4 to 6
PREPARATION: 20 minutes
COOKING: 45 minutes

This outstanding combination is delicious served hot or at room temperature.

3 medium zucchini, sliced ⅛ inch thick
4 medium red-skinned potatoes, sliced ⅛ inch thick
2 medium eggplants, sliced ⅛ inch thick
1 large red pepper, cored, seeded, and thinly sliced
1 large onion, peeled and thinly sliced
3 garlic cloves, finely chopped
1 teaspoon dried oregano
1 teaspoon dried marjoram
½ teaspoon dried thyme
4 tablespoons chopped fresh parsley
Salt
Freshly ground pepper
Olive oil
Red wine vinegar (optional)

■ Preheat the oven to 350°F.

■ Combine the vegetables, garlic, and herbs in a roasting pan large enough to hold the vegetable slices in an overlapping layer. Season with salt and pepper, drizzle on enough oil to coat the vegetables generously, and toss thoroughly. Arrange the vegetables in overlapping rows, and press them down with your hands.

■ Roast the vegetables about 45 minutes, or until they are tender and the edges are crisply browned.

■ Serve the vegetables warm or at room temperature, and sprinkle with a few drops of red wine vinegar if you like.

Note: The vegetables also may be cooked on the grill. After tossing the vegetables with the oil and seasonings, divide them among several large sheets of heavy aluminum foil, allowing plenty of margin to make a tightly sealed package. Enclose the vegetables in the foil, fold the edges, then place on the cooler edge of the grill to cook for about 40 minutes.

Pecan Moons

MAKES ABOUT 24 cookies
PREPARATION: 15 minutes plus chilling time
COOKING: 10 minutes

We're over the moon about these crisp, delicate cookies.

¾ cup (1½ sticks) unsalted butter, softened
½ cup confectioners' sugar
1 teaspoon vanilla extract
2 cups all-purpose flour
1 cup coarsely chopped pecans
Confectioners' sugar (optional)

■ Combine the butter and ½ cup confectioners' sugar in a bowl and beat until smooth. Add the vanilla. Stir in the flour and mix until a dough begins to form. Add the pecans and continue working the mixture until all ingredients are fully incorporated.

■ Shape the dough into a log about 1½ inches thick and place on a sheet of wax paper or foil. Wrap the dough tightly, using the paper or foil to help form the dough into a cylinder. Chill the dough at least 30 minutes, or until firm.

■ Preheat the oven to 325°F.

■ Unwrap the dough and slice it into ¼-inch-thick rounds. Place the rounds ½ inch apart on a baking sheet.

■ Bake until the cookies are lightly browned around the edges, about 10 minutes.

■ Allow the cookies to cool slightly, then loosen carefully with a spatula and allow to cool completely. If desired, sift confectioners' sugar over the cookies.

■ Layer the cookies, separated by sheets of wax paper, in an airtight container.

"For centuries the notion has persisted that the Captain is in charge of his ship. But this is merely a myth, a thin facade of law and custom. The Cook is the Captain, and he always has been."

Neil Hollander and Harald Mertes

Bequia Barbecue

MENU

Tropical Drinks

Grilled Ginger Chicken

Green Bean and Tomato Salad

Rice and Pea Salad

Fresh Lime Pie

■

The tiny Caribbean island of Bequia, accessible only by boat, is steeped in a rich boat-building and whaling tradition. Boats are raised on the beach in the shade of palm trees, and Bequian sailors still rely on harpoons, oars, and 28-foot open whale-boats to hunt from the last week of January to the first week of May. When a whale is captured, the carcass is towed to nearby Petit Nevis, where a village elder divides the meat among island families. Then there's a big party with a steel band, dancing, and free-flowing rum.

Last November we missed the whaling season but found Admiralty Bay, with its

LEFT TO RIGHT: Hearty rice and pea salad; colorful salad of local green beans and tomatoes; mahogany-colored pumpkin and local bread brushed with olive oil on the grill; succulent marinated chicken legs on a bed of shredded cabbage.

 ABOVE: We found this beautiful view while hiking in the hills above Admiralty Bay.

gentle green hills sheltering the harbor, a lovely place to anchor. We quickly succumbed to Bequia's unhurried life-style, and spent several days windsurfing, exploring, or simply loafing when it became too hot to move. And we soon discovered that hot, sunny days call for cool, refreshing drinks in abundance.

The heat not only induced the sluggardly symptoms of a condition known as "going tropo" but drove us to devise meals that involved minimal cooking. As in the following menu, one dinner featured a chicken marinade with ginger root and a few shots of the local rum. A trip to the vegetable stand near the quay yielded pale green pigeon peas, irregularly shaped but dead ripe tomatoes, and knobby green beans much like Italian flat beans. While we prepared dinner, enterprising local boys in handmade skiffs rowed alongside, selling everything from serenades to the West Indian limes that we fashioned into a quick Key lime pie.

Grilled Ginger Chicken

SERVES 6
PREPARATION: 15 minutes plus 1 hour
  marinating
COOKING: 30 minutes

We concocted this zippy marinade to enhance the flavor of the frozen chicken found in many Caribbean supermarkets.

5 pounds chicken legs
2 to 3 garlic cloves, chopped or pressed
2 teaspoons salt
4 tablespoons freshly squeezed lime juice
  (about 3 limes)
2 tablespoons Worcestershire sauce
1/4 cup rum
1 tablespoon brown sugar
1/2 inch piece ginger root, finely chopped
1/4 cup vegetable oil

■ Defrost the chicken and dry with a paper towel. Rub the chicken with garlic and salt and place in a nonmetallic dish or heavy plastic bag. Combine the remaining ingredients and add to the chicken. Marinate in a cool place at least 1 hour, or refrigerate up to 2 days.

■ Prepare the grill (page 13).

■ When coals are medium hot cook chicken legs, turning the pieces after about 10 minutes and basting them frequently with the marinade for a total of about 30 minutes, until they are golden brown. If the chicken is browning too quickly, move to a cooler part of the grill.

■ Serve hot or at room temperature.

Suggested Wine: A tart, spicy white wine such as a California or Alsatian Gewürztraminer.

Spiced Roast Chicken
(ALTERNATE RECIPE)

SERVES 4 to 6
PREPARATION: 20 minutes plus 1 hour
  marinating
COOKING: 30 minutes

3 pounds chicken parts
1 teaspoon salt
1/4 cup freshly squeezed lemon or lime juice
1 tablespoon cumin seeds
1 tablespoon sweet paprika
1/2 teaspoon crushed red pepper
2 garlic cloves, finely chopped
1/3 cup olive oil

■ Rub the chicken with salt and place in a large shallow dish. Add the remaining ingredients and turn the chicken until it is coated evenly. Cover and set aside to marinate for at least 1 hour.

■ Prepare the grill (page 13).

■ Cook the chicken over medium heat, turning the pieces after about 10 minutes and basting them frequently with the marinade for a total of about 30 minutes, or until they are golden brown. (If the chicken is browning too quickly, move to a cooler part of the grill.)

■ Serve hot or at room temperature.

"I drink she every day. She my fountain of youth juice."
100-year-old Bequian, speaking of whale oil

Variation: Make a bed of sliced potatoes in an oiled baking pan. Place the chicken and the marinade on top of the potatoes in one uncrowded layer. Bake, basting occasionally with the pan juices, in a 350°F. oven about 1 hour, or until chicken is browned and tender.

Green Bean and Tomato Salad

SERVES 4 to 6
PREPARATION: 10 minutes
COOKING: 10 minutes

This simple salad goes well with grilled meats or other salads. Use the best quality oil and vinegar available.

1 pound green beans, trimmed
Olive oil
1 tablespoon red wine vinegar
Salt
Freshly ground pepper
2 to 3 ripe tomatoes, halved, seeded, and
    cut into ½-inch pieces
½ medium red onion, thinly sliced

■ Cook the beans in boiling salted water or a steamer until tender but slightly crisp and bright green. Cool beans by immersing them in cold water —sea water is fine—then drain well and shake off excess moisture.

■ In a large bowl, toss the beans with 2 to 3 tablespoons oil. Sprinkle with vinegar and season to taste with salt and pepper.

■ Transfer the beans to a serving dish and scatter the tomatoes and onions on top.

Rice and Pea Salad

SERVES 4 to 6
PREPARATION: 15 minutes
COOKING: 30 minutes

Pigeon peas, a Caribbean staple, are usually shelled by women in the open markets and sold by the bag. Cooked with rice and dressed with vinaigrette, they are a flavorful accompaniment to grilled meats.

1 bay leaf
1 teaspoon salt
½ pound shelled pigeon peas
1 cup uncooked long-grain rice
1 garlic clove, finely chopped or pressed
2 to 3 scallions, thinly sliced (or substitute
    thinly sliced red or yellow onion)
3 to 4 tablespoons vinegar or freshly
    squeezed lime juice
1 to 2 fresh chiles, seeded and finely
    chopped
5 to 6 tablespoons vegetable oil
Salt

■ Bring 2 quarts water to a boil and add the bay leaf and salt. Add the peas and cook 10 minutes.

■ Sprinkle the rice over the peas and cook, stirring occasionally, until the rice is tender but still firm, about 15 minutes.

■ Drain the peas and rice in a large sieve and place in a large bowl. Spread the mixture along the bottom and sides of the bowl to cool it quickly. Remove and discard the bay leaf.

■ Add the remaining ingredients and toss. Season with additional salt if desired.

POWER PUNCH
■

After enjoying several rum punches in a Bequia bar, we persuaded the barman to part with his recipe, which he gave to us in this jingle:

One of sour,
Two of sweet,
Three of strong,
Four of weak.

In other words, mix together 1 part fresh lime juice, 2 parts sugar syrup, 3 parts rum, and 4 parts fruit juices (pineapple, grapefruit, orange, passionfruit, or guava.). Not mentioned in the jingle is the delicious fresh nutmeg grated sparingly on top of the drink. Some bartenders also add a dash of Angostura bitters or a shot of Grenadine syrup, while others prefer a mixture of light and dark rum.

Fresh Lime Pie

MAKES one 8- or 9-inch pie
PREPARATION: 30 minutes
COOKING: 25 minutes

If you are able to find the small, yellowish Key limes, try them in this recipe for a special treat.

Graham Cracker Crust
2 cups graham cracker crumbs (about 11 graham crackers) or other crisp cookie crumbs
2 tablespoons sugar
1/2 cup (1 stick) unsalted butter, melted

Filling
1 14-ounce can sweetened condensed milk
1/2 cup freshly squeezed lime juice (about 6 small limes)
Grated rind of 1 lime (about 1 teaspoon)
2 eggs, separated
1/2 teaspoon vanilla extract
1 tablespoon sugar

■ Preheat the oven to 325°F.

■ To make the crust, place the crackers in a heavy plastic bag and, using a rolling pin or bottle, crush them.

■ Place the crumbs in a bowl. Stir in the sugar and melted butter. Press the mixture into an 8- or 9-inch pie pan and chill about 15 minutes. Bake the pie shell until it is firm and crisp, about 10 minutes.

■ To make the filling, whisk the condensed milk, lime juice, and lime rind in a bowl until blended. Add the egg yolks and vanilla and beat until smooth and thick.

■ In a separate bowl, beat the whites until they hold soft peaks. Sprinkle the sugar on the whites and continue beating until stiff. Fold the whites into the lime mixture and turn into the prepared shell.

■ Bake until the filling is set, about 15 minutes. Cool.

Variations: Combine 1 cup heavy cream and 2 tablespoons confectioners' sugar in a bowl and beat until stiff. Spread the cream over the cooled filling and chill until ready to serve.

Mix together 1 cup sour cream, 1/3 cup sugar, and 1 teaspoon of vanilla and spread on the warm pie. Return the pie to the oven for 5 minutes, then chill.

For a fast unbaked dessert, mix the lime juice with the condensed milk, stir until thick, and serve in small cups or glasses with a dollop of whipped cream, yogurt, or sour cream. Garnish with fresh berries.

Strawberry Daiquiri

MAKES 3 drinks

2 ounces Triple Sec
4 ounces Tequila
1/4 cup freshly squeezed lime juice (about 3 limes)
1/4 cup sugar
1 pint fresh strawberries, hulled and halved, or one 10-ounce package frozen strawberries, partially defrosted
1 cup crushed ice
Lime slices
Fresh whole strawberries (optional)

■ Purée the ingredients in a blender until smooth.

■ Pour into wine or Tom Collins glasses and serve immediately with a slice of lime and a whole fresh strawberry.

Lime Syrup

MAKES ABOUT 4 cups

This syrup may be used for limeade, a refreshing thirst quencher, or made into more potent concoctions.

2 cups fresh lime juice (about 12 large limes)
1 cup sugar
1½ cups water

■ Strain the lime juice and refrigerate.

■ Combine the sugar and water in a saucepan and bring to a boil over high heat. Reduce the heat to low and simmer, stirring until the sugar dissolves.

■ Cool the syrup and combine with the juice.

Note: To make limeade, combine the syrup with 3 cups cold water and mix well. Pour the liquid into a large pitcher filled with ice and garnish with thin slices of lime. Makes 10 servings.

Banana Liquado

MAKES 1 drink

A smooth Mexican-style fruit drink.

1 medium banana
½ cup plain yogurt
½ cup pineapple juice
1 tablespoon brown sugar or honey
1 tablespoon freshly squeezed lime or lemon juice
3 to 4 ice cubes

■ Combine ingredients in a blender at high speed until smooth.

■ Serve immediately.

Note: Fruits such as papaya, melon, peaches, or berries also work well.

Banana Blast

MAKES 2 drinks

3 ounces light rum
¼ cup cream of coconut
1 medium ripe banana
1 cup pineapple juice
1 cup crushed ice

■ Combine ingredients in a blender at high speed until smooth.

■ Serve immediately.

Fresh flowers and fruit add a luxurious flair to tropical drinks.

Late Summer Fête

M E N U

Grated Gazpacho

Grilled Marinated Tuna

Couscous

Green Salad

Fresh Melon

■

By August we have surrendered to the intense pleasures of summer, spending as much time as possible swimming, sailing, windsurfing, and generally indulging in the salty joys of the water. Tanned and relaxed, we turn to casual menus that celebrate carefree outdoor living.

On hot nights, cold dishes and sizzling barbecues remain our favorites. With summer comes a bounty of fresh garden vegetables and fish from the sea that deserve to be prepared in uncomplicated ways. In the following menu, cool gazpacho bursts with the full flavors of tomatoes, cucumbers, and peppers. Skewered chunks of tuna gain succulence from a robust red-wine marinade. Lush ripe melon is a refreshing conclusion to this warm-weather meal, reminding us how good food tastes in the summertime.

Grated Gazpacho

SERVES 4 to 6

PREPARATION: 20 minutes

Some gazpacho fans add a glass of dry sherry to this soup or serve it with little bowls of chopped vegetables. If you are blessed with a blender, ignore the instructions below and whirl the vegetables into a puree.

3 cucumbers
3 to 4 large ripe tomatoes
2 or 3 green and red bell peppers
1 medium mild onion
2 garlic cloves, finely chopped
3 to 4 cups tomato juice or V-8
¼ cup red wine vinegar
¼ cup olive oil
Tabasco
Salt
Chopped fresh basil, parsley, or tarragon (optional)

Garnish
Croutons

■ Peel the cucumbers, cut them in half lengthwise, and scoop out the seeds. Grate the cucumbers coarsely into a large bowl.

■ Cut the tomatoes in half crosswise and scoop out the seeds. Coarsely grate each half into the bowl, cut side down, until only the skin remains. Discard the skin.

■ Core and seed the peppers, then grate them flesh side down, discarding the skin. Grate the onion into the bowl.

■ Stir in the garlic, tomato juice, vinegar, and oil. Season to taste with Tabasco and salt. Put the soup into a Thermos with 3 or 4 ice cubes.

■ If available, stir in chopped herbs. Serve with crisp croutons.

Grilled Marinated Tuna

SERVES 6

PREPARATION: 20 minutes plus 30 minutes marinating

COOKING: 10 minutes

This lusty marinade also goes well with swordfish or shark.

2½ to 3 pounds fresh tuna
2 garlic cloves, crushed
1 medium onion, finely chopped
1 teaspoon dried oregano or marjoram
1 teaspoon coarsely ground pepper
1½ cups robust red or dry white wine
½ cup olive oil
1 bay leaf
1 2-inch strip orange rind
*2 to 3 medium zucchini, cut crosswise
   into ½-inch rounds*

■ Trim away any dark red portions of the tuna. Cut the tuna into 1½-inch squares and place in a nonmetallic bowl.

■ Add the garlic, onion, oregano, and pepper and toss well, rubbing the seasonings into the fish. Add the wine, oil, bay leaf, and orange rind, and turn the fish to coat with this mixture. Marinate for 30 minutes at room temperature.

■ Prepare the grill (page 13).

■ Thread alternating pieces of the tuna and zucchini snugly on skewers.

■ Grill about 5 minutes on each side, brushing occasionally with the reserved marinade, until lightly browned. Serve immediately.

Suggested Wine: An earthy red wine such as a Spanish Rioja or a light California Zinfandel.

Barbequed Fish with Potatoes and Vegetables
(ALTERNATE RECIPE)

SERVES 4 to 6
PREPARATION: 30 minutes plus 15
   minutes marinating
COOKING: 40 minutes

A whole grill-roasted fish surrounded by savory glistening vegetables is an impressive sight. This recipe works best with firm-fleshed fish such as grouper, pompano, sea trout, or red snapper.

*1 whole grouper (4½ to 5 pounds),
   cleaned, with head and tail intact, or
   2 2- to 3-pound grouper*
Salt
Paprika
1 garlic clove, finely chopped
1 teaspoon dried oregano
Olive oil
*6 tablespoons freshly squeezed lemon
   juice (about 2 lemons)*
*4 to 6 medium potatoes, peeled and sliced
   ⅛ inch thick*
1 medium onion, thinly sliced
*2 to 3 firm ripe tomatoes, cored and sliced
   ¼ inch thick*
*2 medium cucumbers, peeled and sliced
   ⅛ inch thick*
2 oranges, sliced ⅛ inch thick

■ With a sharp knife, cut 3 or 4 parallel crosswise slashes about ¼ inch deep on each side of the fish.

■ Rub the fish with salt, paprika, garlic, and oregano. Drizzle on the oil and lemon juice and rub into the fish, pushing the seasonings into the slashes. Marinate for about 15 minutes.

■ Prepare the grill (page 13).

■ Place an 18-inch square of heavy foil on top of second square of equal size. Oil the top sheet. Arrange the potato and onion slices in an overlapping layer on the foil, leaving a 4-inch margin all around. Sprinkle with salt, paprika, and about 2 tablespoons of oil.

■ Place the fish on the vegetables. Cover with overlapping slices of tomato and cucumber, then sprinkle them with salt and drizzle with oil. Finish with a layer of orange slices. Enclose the fish in the foil, folding over the edges to form a tight seal.

■ Place the package on the grill, cover, and cook until the fish tests done and the potatoes are tender, about 40 minutes.

■ To serve, carefully unwrap the package and slide the fish and vegetables onto a platter.

Suggested Wine: A crisp, white Rhône or a lighter-bodied red such as Chianti or a light Zinfandel.

GRILLING FISH
■
If you've hooked a fish and want to grill it whole, you can easily do so. First lay a sheet of heavy foil on the grill, tucking under the edges. Punch holes in the foil about 1 inch apart. When the fire is ready, brush the foil with oil and place the cleaned fish on it. Measure the fish at the thickest part and plan to cook 10 minutes per inch. Midway through the cooking time, turn the fish and test every 5 minutes. To keep the fish juicy, remove it from the heat slightly undercooked, since the fish will continue to cook off the heat for a few minutes.

TOP: Tuna and zucchini skewers ready for the grill. **A**BOVE: Luscious ripe melon for dessert.

RIGHT: An informal summer feast in the cockpit. The antique dolphin candlesticks add a whimsical note.

This is a Swell Ship for the Skipper, but a Hell Ship for the crew

Couscous

SERVES 6
PREPARATION: 15 minutes

Couscous can be made in minutes and is ideal for galley cooking.

1¾ cups chicken broth or water
½ teaspoon salt
1 2-inch strip orange or lemon rind (optional)
1⅔ cup instant couscous
4 tablespoons (½ stick) unsalted butter

Garnish
Sliced oranges
Sliced almonds
Chopped fresh parsley

■ Bring the chicken broth to a boil in a large saucepan over high heat. Add the salt, orange rind, couscous, and butter. Cover and cook for about 1 minute. Remove the pan from the heat and, without removing the cover, allow the couscous to stand about 10 minutes, or until the water is fully absorbed.

■ Fluff the couscous lightly with a fork and turn into a serving dish. Discard the orange rind. If desired, surround with sliced oranges and sprinkle with sliced almonds and chopped parsley.

Couscous Salad

(ALTERNATE RECIPE)

SERVES 4 to 6
PREPARATION: 25 minutes

A cool summer salad that can be prepared up to a day in advance.

1⅔ cups instant couscous
3 tablespoons currants
1 2-inch piece of orange rind
1¾ cups water
½ cup finely chopped fresh parsley
3 scallions, thinly sliced
4 to 5 tablespoons freshly squeezed lemon juice
6 tablespoons olive oil
Salt

■ Place the couscous, currants, and orange rind in a large mixing bowl. Heat the water to boiling and add to the couscous. Cover the bowl and let stand 15 minutes, or until the water is absorbed.

■ Remove the orange rind and fluff the couscous with a fork. Fold in the remaining ingredients and season to taste with salt.

Green Salad

SERVES 6
PREPARATION: 15 minutes

We like green salads dressed simply with good olive oil and vinegar, using a ration of 3 or 4 parts oil to 1 part vinegar.

8 cups mixed greens such as Romaine and iceberg lettuce, chicory, and Belgian endive

Vinaigrette
1 teaspoon Dijon mustard
2 to 3 tablespoons red or white wine vinegar
2 tablespoons olive oil
¼ cup vegetable oil
Salt
Freshly ground pepper

■ Tear the greens into bite-size pieces and place in a large bowl.

■ Combine the vinaigrette ingredients in a small bowl and whisk thoroughly. Pour the vinaigrette over the greens and toss lightly.

Fresh Melon

SERVES 6 to 8
PREPARATION: 10 minutes

■ Cut a ripe 3-pound melon, such as cantaloupe or honeydew, in half and scoop out the seeds. Cut the halves lengthwise into ¾-inch-wide crescents. Cut off and discard the rind. Cut each piece in half crosswise.

■ Arrange the melon on a plate, sprinkle with sherry if desired, and garnish with lime wedges.

We favor all-green salads and often mix several types, using a larger amount of milder greens with smaller portions of more pungent ones. Some successful combinations:

· Romaine lettuce, endive, and radicchio

· Romaine lettuce, chicory, arugula, and parsley

· Iceberg lettuce, parsley, and celery leaves

· Escarole, Romaine lettuce, sprouted lentils, and walnuts

· Watercress, Boston lettuce, arugula, basil, coriander, and mint

Dinner Aboard Aphrodite

In the glory days of yachting, multimillionaire John Hay Whitney was the proud owner of *Aphrodite,* a magnificent mahogany powerboat he used to commute during summers from his Greentree estate in Manhasset, Long Island, to his Wall Street office.

Hopping aboard weekday mornings in his pajamas, Whitney would shower on the sleek 74-foot yacht, have his breakfast and newspaper served to him by a steward, and arrive at the bustling tip of lower Manhattan in less than forty-five minutes. From her maiden voyage in 1937 *Aphrodite* was a legend on Long Island Sound, and her clipper bow and buxom stern were recognized by boat aficionados everywhere. Shirley Temple and Jennifer Jones were guests for dinner. Fred Astaire danced on her decks.

Today *Aphrodite* has been lovingly restored to her original splendor by a young couple who seem unperturbed by the logistics of living on a boat with an energetic three-year-old and a newborn baby. They love to entertain and delight guests by serving candlelight dinners in the glistening boathouse, where an elegant table is set with *Aphrodite*'s original gold-leafed Minton china, engraved flatware, and antique crystal.

Grilled Filet of Beef with Mushroom Sauce

SERVES 8 to 10
PREPARATION: 20 minutes
COOKING: 25 to 35 minutes

1 4-pound beef filet, trimmed of all fat
Olive oil
Salt
Freshly ground pepper

■ Preheat the oven to 450°F. or prepare the grill (page 13).

■ Roll the filet and tie it with string at 1½-inch intervals. Rub with oil, salt, and pepper.

■ If using an oven, roast the filet in a pan about 25 minutes for rare. If using a grill, cook it about 30 minutes, turning frequently.

■ Prepare the mushroom sauce while the beef cooks.

DINNERS AFLOAT

TOP: *Aphrodite* martini glasses from the 1930s. LEFT: Grilled filet of beef with shiitake mushrooms served on original *Aphrodite* china. OPPOSITE: Waterford crystal, antique flatware, and fresh flowers create a refined mood.

An elegant evening brought to a close with delicate crêpes, strong French roast, and a fine liqueur.

Mushroom Sauce

MAKES 3 cups
PREPARATION: 15 minutes
COOKING: 15 minutes

2 tablespoons unsalted butter
1 tablespoon olive oil
1 garlic clove, finely chopped
1/2 teaspoon dried thyme
1/2 teaspoon dried marjoram
1 pound fresh button or shiitake
   mushrooms with stems removed, sliced,
   or 6 ounces dried shiitake mushrooms,
   soaked in warm water, drained,
   trimmed, and sliced
Salt
Freshly ground pepper
1/2 cup beef broth
1 cup dry red wine

■ Heat the butter and oil in a large skillet over medium-high heat.

■ When the butter is foaming, add the garlic and herbs. Stir until the garlic is fragrant. Add the mushrooms and toss to coat with the butter and herb mixture. Reduce the heat to medium and cook, covered, stirring occasionally, until the mushrooms have softened and are beginning to brown, about 5 minutes.

■ Season the mushrooms with salt and pepper, and add the broth and wine. Bring to a boil and cook, stirring occasionally, about 5 minutes, or until the liquid is reduced by half and the sauce is slightly thickened.

Suggested Wine: A rich, robust red such as a California Merlot or Cabernet Sauvignon.

Buttered Cabbage with Scallions

SERVES 4
PREPARATION: 10 minutes
COOKING: 10 minutes

These tender triangles of cabbage are scented with a sweet hint of orange.

2 tablespoons unsalted butter
1/2 medium cabbage, cut into bite-size
   triangles (about 5 cups)
Salt
1/4 cup orange juice
2 to 3 scallions, thinly sliced

■ Melt the butter in a skillet over medium heat. Add the cabbage, salt lightly, and toss for a few minutes. Add the orange juice, cover the pan, and cook about 5 minutes, stirring occasionally. Add the scallions.

■ Cover and cook 5 minutes longer, or until tender.

Gratin of Sweet and White Potatoes

SERVES 4 to 6
PREPARATION: 20 minutes
COOKING: 30 minutes

Aluminum foil expands the possibilities for shipboard cooking. Here it is used to steam vegetables on the grill.

4 to 6 tablespoons olive oil or melted
   unsalted butter
3 large white potatoes, peeled and sliced
   1/8 inch thick
3 large yellow sweet potatoes, peeled and
   sliced 1/8 inch thick
Salt
Freshly ground pepper
Fresh or dried thyme
2 or 3 garlic cloves, crushed

■ Prepare the grill (page 13).

■ Place several long, 18-inch-wide sheets of aluminum foil on a work surface. Brush each sheet with oil or butter. Closely lap alternating rows of potatoes in the center of each piece of the foil, leaving sufficient margins to enclose the vegetables. Drizzle the remaining oil over the vegetables. Sprinkle lightly with salt, pepper, and thyme and place the garlic on top.

■ Enclose the vegetables in the foil,

folding over the edges of each packet several times to make a sturdy seal.

■ Place the foil packets on the edges of the grill to prevent burning. After 20 to 30 minutes, test the vegetables through the foil for tenderness with a skewer or ice pick. (Resist the temptation to puncture the foil too soon, once the seal is broken, the steam will escape.)

Note: If you don't have a grill, layer alternating slices of the vegetables in a shallow baking dish and bake for 30 minutes at 400°F. Vegetables prepared this way will be nicely browned.

Orange Crêpes with Strawberry Sauce

SERVES 4 to 6
PREPARATION: 10 minutes plus 1 hour
  to allow the crêpe batter to rest
COOKING: 30 minutes

A light and elegant way to end a meal.

Crêpes
3 large eggs
1 to 1¼ cups milk
⅛ teaspoon salt
½ cup all-purpose flour
3 tablespoons unsalted butter, melted,
  plus additional for assembly
Vegetable oil

Orange Butter
4 tablespoons (½ stick) unsalted butter,
  softened
¼ cup sugar
1 teaspoon grated orange rind
1 tablespoon orange liqueur such as
  Cointreau or Triple Sec

Strawberry Sauce
1 pint fresh strawberries
2 to 3 tablespoons sugar
¼ cup orange liqueur such as Cointreau
  or Triple Sec

■ Whisk the eggs in a medium mixing bowl with 1 cup milk and the salt until blended. Add the flour gradually, whisking until smooth. Strain the batter through a wire sieve, then stir in the 3 tablespoons melted butter.

■ Cover the crêpe batter and let stand 1 hour at room temperature. (The batter should have the consistency of heavy cream. If it is too thick, thin with a little milk or water.)

■ Heat a 6- or 7-inch omelet or crêpe pan over medium-high heat. Add a teaspoon of vegetable oil and rub the pan with a paper towel, leaving a thin film of oil. Hold the pan at an angle and add about 2 tablespoons of the crêpe batter. Tilt the pan, using a rolling motion to coat the surface evenly with the batter. Return any excess batter to the bowl.

■ Cook the crêpe about 30 seconds until the edge curls. Turn the crêpe with your fingertips. Cook the other side for about 15 seconds, then slip it onto a plate. Cook the remaining batter in the same manner, stirring the batter gently before pouring each crêpe. Stack the crêpes to keep them from drying out.

■ To make the Orange Butter, combine the butter, sugar, and orange rind in a bowl and beat with a wooden spoon until smooth and creamy. Beat in the orange liqueur.

■ To make the Strawberry Sauce, hull the strawberries, rinse in cold water, and drain. Put half the strawberries in a small bowl. Add the sugar and crush the strawberries with a fork to make a chunky sauce. Stir in the orange liqueur. Slice the remaining strawberries and stir into the sauce. Cover and keep cool until ready to serve.

■ To assemble, carefully place the crêpes on the work surface and mound about 2 teaspoons of Orange Butter in the center of each. Fold the crêpes in half, then in half again, to create little triangles, and place in a buttered baking dish in a slightly overlapping layer. Brush the tops of the crêpes lightly with melted butter, then bake about 10 minutes. Serve immediately, placing 2 or 3 crêpes on each dessert plate. Top with a few tablespoons Strawberry Sauce.

Supper in a Quiet Cove

MENU

Mussels with Herbs

French Bread

Chicken Breasts Stuffed with Herbed Cheese

Buttered Carrots and Potatoes

Boston Lettuce Salad

Sliced Oranges with Cinnamon

■

OPPOSITE, CLOCKWISE: **This pretty, refreshing dessert is Mediterranean in origin; crisp, succulent chicken with bright tender vegetables; shiny black mussels ready for steaming.**

With their exquisite lines and brightwork like buckwheat honey, Concordia yawls are the stuff that wooden sailboat fantasies are made of. These classic boats, designed in 1938 to handle a choppy Buzzards Bay sou'wester comfortably, are also a gem to sail, and over time have won more races than boats of any other class. Perhaps the greatest testament to their design integrity is the fact that, of the 103 Concordias made, every one is still being sailed.

While cruising Long Island Sound aboard *Wild Rose,* a graceful Concordia built in 1938, we found a quiet cove near Sag Harbor for the night. Supper was served below and began with succulent mussels gathered from the Sound that morning, followed by chicken breasts stuffed with herbed ricotta cheese. After dinner, we ventured back on deck for coffee, bundled in sweaters against the cool evening air.

Mussels with Herbs

SERVES 6
PREPARATION: 20 minutes
COOKING: 15 minutes

2 tablespoons olive oil
1 medium onion, finely chopped
1 teaspoon dried marjoram or oregano
3 tablespoons chopped fresh parsley
1 garlic clove, finely chopped
½ cup white wine
3 dozen mussels, scrubbed and debearded
French bread

■ Heat the oil in a saucepan large enough to hold the mussels over medium heat, then add the onion and sauté until soft, about 5 minutes. Stir in the herbs and garlic, then add the wine and mussels. Cover the pot and increase the heat to high. Steam until the mussels open, about 5 minutes.

■ With a slotted spoon, transfer the mussels to a large serving bowl, discarding any unopened ones. Pour the cooking juices over the mussels, taking care not to disturb the sandy sediment in the bottom of the pan. Serve immediately with hot French bread to soak up the juices.

Suggested Wine: A crisp, dry white such as Muscadet or a California Sauvignon Blanc.

Chicken Breasts Stuffed with Herbed Cheese

SERVES 6
PREPARATION: 15 minutes
COOKING: 40 minutes

Stuffed under the skin with herbed ricotta, these chicken breasts turn golden brown, while the meat remains moist.

6 boneless chicken breast halves, skin on
Salt
Freshly ground pepper
Lemon juice or white wine
1½ cups ricotta cheese
½ cup freshly grated Parmesan cheese
1 egg
2 tablespoons chopped fresh parsley
1 teaspoon dried marjoram

■ Preheat the oven to 400°F.

■ Season the chicken breasts with salt and pepper and sprinkle with a little lemon juice.

■ Combine the ricotta, Parmesan, egg, and herbs in a small bowl. Beat with a wooden spoon until well blended. Season to taste with salt and pepper.

■ Form a pocket for the stuffing by separating the skin from the chicken with your fingertips, keeping the skin attached along the edges. Push spoonfuls of the cheese stuffing under the skin, packing it generously. Pat the skin to distribute the stuffing evenly. Tuck the edges of the skin under each breast and place them about ½ inch apart in a baking pan large enough to hold them comfortably.

■ Bake the chicken for 10 minutes, then lower the heat to 375°F. and bake about 30 minutes, or until the chicken skin is a deep golden brown.

Suggested wine: A crisp, dry white such as a California Sauvignon Blanc or Italian Orvieto.

Buttered Carrots and Potatoes

MAKES 6 servings
PREPARATION: 10 minutes
COOKING: 15 minutes

4 to 6 carrots, peeled
4 to 6 red potatoes, scrubbed
Unsalted butter or olive oil
Salt
Pepper

■ Cut the carrots and cut into 1-inch pieces. Place the vegetables in a large skillet with about ¼ inch of water. Bring the water to a boil over high heat and cover the pan tightly. Lower the heat to medium and steam the vegetables until they are just tender, about 10 minutes.

■ Uncover the pan and add butter and salt and pepper to taste. Cook, tossing the vegetables, until any remaining moisture evaporates from the pan.

Variation: Add finely sliced scallions or crumbled herbs along with the butter and seasonings.

Sliced Oranges with Cinnamon

SERVES 6
PREPARATION: 20 minutes

6 navel oranges
6 tablespoons orange liqueur such as
    Cointreau or Triple Sec
Confectioners' sugar
Cinnamon

■ Remove a small slice from the bottom of each orange. Stand each orange on end and, with a small, sharp knife, cut away the peel. Cut the oranges crosswise into ⅛-inch-thick slices and arrange in overlapping rows on a serving dish or on individual plates.

■ Drizzle the liqueur over the oranges and sprinkle with sugar and cinnamon.

Fogbound Feast

Some years ago on Martha's Vineyard, we were socked in by a real "pea souper." Boats moored nearby became dim silhouettes in the thick, wet mist. Channel markers and buoys disappeared. The scratchy morning radio forecast confirmed what we already suspected: no sailing.

Sitting in the clammy galley at breakfast, feeling bored and mutinuous, we decided to make the most of a dreary day: we would create a leisurely, memorable dinner. As we drew up a dinner menu that began with steamers, the food-loving crew became increasingly enthusiastic. Everyone wanted to help. We were delighted; although we'd spent cozy winter afternoons at home cooking with friends, it's unusual on a boat, where everyone wants to be outdoors.

Donning slickers, a few of us rowed ashore to buy groceries in town, while others headed down the beach with pails and rakes in search of clams. Gathering back in the cabin several hours later, people cracked open cold beers and steamed mounds of clams. The bread warming in the oven dispelled the cabin dampness. Everyone devoured the juicy steamers dripping with butter while dinner simmered on the stove. The flickering glow of a kerosene lamp completed the warm, cozy atmosphere.

Later, with everyone stuffed and satisfied, we agreed that the dinner on Martha's Vineyard was one of the best on the cruise. But it was the camaraderie of creating our fogbound feast that remained in people's memories long after the sailing season ended.

Steamers with Bay Leaves

SERVES 4 to 6
PREPARATION: 15 minutes
COOKING: 10 minutes

One of our favorite finger foods. Serve with hot French bread for dunking into the delicious juices.

5 pounds soft-shell clams, scrubbed
1 cup dry white wine
4 or 5 bay leaves
Lemon wedges
Melted butter

■ Put the clams, wine, and bay leaves in a large pot with a tight-fitting lid. Bring the liquid to a boil over high heat and cook until the clams open, about 10 minutes. Scoop the clams into a large bowl, discarding any unopened "mudders," and reserve the broth.

■ Pour the broth into mugs, taking care not to disturb any sediment in the bottom of the pan. Serve the clams with lemon wedges, mugs of steaming broth, and melted butter. Pass a big bowl for the empty shells.

ABOVE: Steamers and beer down below. **R**IGHT: A warming dessert—sautéed apples and pears with hard sauce.

FAR RIGHT: What better way to beat the fog than a cozy supper in the main salon?

Beef Stew with Onions and Beer

SERVES 6 to 8
PREPARATION: 20 minutes
COOKING: 60 minutes

Serve this deeply flavored stew with hot bread or steamed potatoes.

3 pounds chuck steak, sliced ¼ inch thick
Salt
Freshly ground pepper
¼ cup vegetable oil
5 large onions, thinly sliced
1 garlic clove, crushed
1 bay leaf
1 teaspoon dried thyme
2 tablespoons all-purpose flour
1 tablespoon brown sugar
2 12-ounce cans beer (preferably dark)

■ Season the beef with salt and pepper. Heat the oil in a large, deep pan over moderately high heat. Quickly brown the beef in batches, removing the slices as they are done.

■ Add the onions to the pan and reduce the heat to medium. Cover and cook the onions, stirring occasionally, until they are soft and golden brown, about 20 minutes. Add the garlic, bay leaf, thyme, and flour. Cook, stirring, for 5 minutes. Add the sugar and slowly add the beer, stirring constantly.

■ Return the beef to the pan and cook, partially covered, about 1 hour, or until the beef is tender. If desired, raise the heat to high and cook the sauce until it is thickened, about 5 minutes.

Note: To cook the stew in a pressure cooker, brown the beef and onions as described. After returning the beef to the pressure cooker, cover and bring the contents to a boil over high heat. When steam rises from the vent, put on the gauge at 15 pounds of pressure. When the gauge jiggles or the indicator shows the correct pressure has been reached, adjust the heat to low. Cook the stew 25 minutes. Remove the pressure cooker from the heat immediately and place it in cold water to reduce the pressure. Remove the lid. If the lid is resistant, cool the pot a little longer to further reduce the pressure.

Suggested Wine: An earthy, spicy red such as Zinfandel or Côtes du Rhône.

One-Pot Hungarian Chicken with Dumplings
(ALTERNATE RECIPE)

SERVES 4
PREPARATION: 30 minutes
COOKING: 45 minutes

This rust-red chicken stew warms the belly on a chilly night.

1 3- to 4-pound frying chicken, cut up, or
  about 3 pounds chicken pieces
Salt
Freshly ground pepper
2 tablespoons vegetable oil
1 medium onion, chopped
2 medium carrots, peeled and sliced
  ¼ inch thick
2 red or green bell peppers, stemmed,
  seeded, and sliced ¼ inch thick
2 garlic cloves, chopped
3 tablespoons sweet paprika
¼ teaspoon cayenne (ground red) pepper
1 bay leaf
1 teaspoon dried oregano
3 tablespoons all-purpose flour
1 14-ounce can whole tomatoes
1 12-ounce can beer
Dumplings (recipe follows)

■ Season the chicken with salt and pepper. Heat the oil in a skillet over medium-high heat. Add the chicken and brown all over, setting aside pieces as they are done.

■ Lower the heat to medium. Add the onion, carrots, peppers, garlic, paprika, cayenne, bay leaf, and oregano to the pan and cook, stirring frequently, until the vegetables are softened, about 5 minutes. Add the flour and cook, stirring, for 2 minutes. Add the tomatoes and beer and stir, scraping any browned particles stuck to the pan.

PRESSURE COOKING

■

Some people understandably fear pressure cookers, having heard how someone's great-aunt Edith blew a hole in the ceiling with one. But pressure cookers have come a long way since Edith's day. Not only are they safe, but pressure cookers will also cut cooking time, reduce galley heat, and double as a spill-proof saucepan in rough weather. Use pressure cookers to steam vegetables, bake bread, and reduce the cooking time of long-simmered stews and beans.

- Return the chicken to the pan, cover, and cook until tender, about 25 minutes. Skim off the excess fat.

- Make the dumpling batter, and cook as described.

Variations: Add 1 cup chopped ham or 1 pound of cubed boneless pork to the vegetables as they cook.

Stir 1 cup sour cream mixed with 2 tablespoons flour into the sauce before adding the dumplings.

Dumplings

SERVES 4
PREPARATION: 5 minutes
COOKING: 15 minutes

1½ cups all-purpose flour
1 tablespoon baking powder
½ teaspoon salt
¾ cup milk
3 tablespoons vegetable oil or melted unsalted butter
2 to 3 drops Tabasco

- Combine the flour, baking powder, and salt in a mixing bowl. Add the milk, oil, and Tabasco, and stir until the dry ingredients are moistened.

- Drop tablespoonfuls of the dough about 1 inch apart on the surface of the simmering stew. Cover and cook, without lifting the lid, until the dumplings are firm and puffed, about 15 minutes.

Cabbage and Carrot Salad with Walnuts

SERVES 4 to 6
PREPARATION: 15 minutes

3 tablespoons wine or cider vinegar
1 teaspoon Dijon mustard
⅓ cup vegetable oil
½ large head green cabbage, thinly sliced
2 carrots, peeled and coarsely grated
½ cup coarsely chopped, lightly toasted walnuts
Salt
Freshly ground pepper

- Combine the vinegar, mustard, and oil in a large salad bowl. Whisk well and add the cabbage, carrots, and half the walnuts.

- Season to taste with salt and pepper, toss well, and sprinkle with the remaining walnuts.

Sautéed Apples and Pears with Hard Sauce

SERVES 4 to 6
PREPARATION: 10 minutes
COOKING: 15 MINUTES

3 apples, cored, quartered, and cut into ½-inch wedges
3 pears, cored and quartered
1 tablespoon freshly squeezed lemon juice
2 tablespoons unsalted butter
2 tablespoons brown sugar
⅛ teaspoon cinnamon
2 tablespoons rum
Hard Sauce (recipe follows)

- Toss the apples and pears with the lemon juice.

- Heat the butter in a large skillet over medium-high heat. When the butter is foaming, add the fruit in one layer. Cook, shaking the pan to keep the fruit from sticking, until the fruit is lightly browned. Turn the fruit pieces carefully and brown the other side. Sprinkle the sugar, cinnamon, and rum over the fruit and cook until the pan juices bubble and thicken. Serve with Hard Sauce.

Hard Sauce

MAKES ABOUT 1 cup
PREPARATION: 10 minutes

3 tablespoons unsalted butter, softened
1 cup confectioners' sugar
1 tablespoon rum
2 tablespoons heavy cream or milk

- Beat the butter in a small mixing bowl until creamy. Add the sugar gradually, beating constantly until smooth. Stir in the rum and cream and mix well.

"Later my financial position improved, and I bought rum, which solved most of my drinking problems. It also made my cooking taste better."

Francis Brenton

Cozy Cabin Dinner

MENU

*Michael's Pork and
Black Bean Chili*

Corn Bread

*Green Salad
(page 32)*

Sliced Tomatoes

Banana Crisp

■

OPPOSITE: **Soul-warming spicy chili is perfect on a cold Maine night.**

Y ou want to sail *when?*" The charter agent thought we were crazy. In Maine, where locals chuckle about the five good swimming days each summer, the boating season doesn't begin until July 1—which is precisely why we wanted to go sailing in May.

Leaving from Boothbay Harbor on Memorial Day weekend (with the charter agent's earnest reassurances that we could have our money back if we returned early, wet, and miserable from the cold), we spent three glorious days cruising the Maine coast. Despite the condominiums crowding the shoreline, the outer islands remain deserted and wild. Sailing from one to another, we saw seals basking on rocks and ospreys building enormous nests. While exploring one island, we even sent a startled porcupine scurrying up a tree.

Our first night out was crisp and cool —perfect for a cozy cabin dinner. People gravitated to the spicy smells of chili simmering on the stove. Soon everyone was chopping, stirring, or sampling. Sequestered in the cabin, we made a leisurely evening of the meal, with no one quite remembering when the preparations ended and the eating began.

Michael's Pork and Black Bean Chili

SERVES 6 to 8
PREPARATION: 20 minutes
COOKING: 2 hours

This recipe comes from our friend Michael McLaughlin, whose superb very spicy chili can be assembled in short order, then left to simmer unattended. Serve the chili with freshly cooked rice, grated cheese, salsa, and chopped or pickled onions.

¼ cup olive oil or vegetable oil
2 medium yellow onions, coarsely chopped
5 garlic cloves, finely chopped
*2½ pounds boneless pork butt, cut into
    ½-inch cubes*
⅓ cup chili powder
1½ tablespoons ground cumin
1½ tablespoons dried oregano
*½ teaspoon cayenne (ground red) pepper,
    or to taste*
1½ teaspoons salt
*1 16-ounce can plum tomatoes, chopped,
    with their juice*
3 cups chicken broth
2 16-ounce cans black beans

■ Heat half the oil in a large skillet over medium heat. Add the onions and garlic and cook, partially covered, until tender, about 20 minutes.

■ Heat the remaining oil in a large, heavy casserole over medium-high heat.

Add the pork and cook, stirring occasionally, until the meat has lost its pink color, about 15 minutes.

■ Stir in the chili powder, cumin, oregano, cayenne, and salt and cook, stirring, for about 2 minutes. Add the onions and garlic, tomatoes, and chicken broth. Bring the chili to a boil, stirring occasionally, then reduce the heat to low and simmer until the pork is tender, about 1½ hours. Taste and adjust the seasonings.

■ Drain the beans, rinse them, and drain well again. Stir the beans into the chili and simmer for 10 minutes.

Note: Cook the pork and onion mixture in a pressure cooker for about 25 minutes; then add the beans.

Corn Bread

SERVES 2 to 4
PREPARATION: 10 minutes
COOKING: 25 minutes

This pristine southern-style corn bread is best eaten hot from the pan.

1 cup white or yellow cornmeal
½ teaspoon baking soda
½ teaspoon salt
1 large egg
¾ cup milk or plain yogurt
¼ cup vegetable oil or melted butter

■ Combine the dry ingredients in a bowl. Make a well in the center and break the egg into it. Beat the egg lightly with a fork, then add the milk and half the oil and incorporate with a few swift strokes.

■ Heat a heavy 10- to 12-inch cast-iron skillet over moderate heat. When the skillet is hot, pour in the remaining oil and heat until it shimmers. Pour in the batter. When the sizzling stops, cover the skillet and turn the heat to low. Cook until the edges of the corn bread brown and the top is dry to the touch, about 15 minutes. Slide a spatula under the bread and turn. Cook until the bread springs back when touched, about 5 minutes.

Hearty Minestrone
(ALTERNATE RECIPE)

SERVES 6 generously
PREPARATION: 30 minutes
COOKING: about 60 minutes

Thick with fresh vegetables and spicy sausages, this mouthwatering soup improves with age.

2 tablespoons olive oil
1 pound hot Portuguese or Italian
   sausage, sliced
1 large onion, coarsely chopped
2 carrots, sliced
1 celery stalk with leaves, sliced
1 or 2 garlic cloves, chopped
½ teaspoon dried thyme
½ teaspoon dried rosemary
1 teaspoon sweet paprika
½ large head of green cabbage, shredded
2 large potatoes, scrubbed and cut into
   ½-inch chunks
1 16-ounce can crushed tomatoes
2 16-ounce cans kidney beans, cannellini
   or pinto beans, or chick-peas
8 cups water or chicken broth
1 pound small tortellini, ravioli,
   agnolotti or other stuffed pasta, cooked
Grated Parmesan, Asiago, or Romano
   cheese

■ Heat the oil in a large soup pot over medium heat. Add the sausage, onion, carrots, celery, garlic, thyme, rosemary, and paprika. Cook, stirring, until the vegetables are softened and the sausage begins to brown. Add the cabbage and potatoes and cook, partially covered, stirring occasionally, until the cabbage is wilted, about 5 minutes.

■ Raise the heat to high and add the crushed tomatoes, beans, and water. When the soup comes to a boil, lower the heat and simmer, stirring occasionally, until the vegetables are tender, about 40 minutes. Add the pasta and simmer for 10 minutes. Serve with grated cheese.

Suggested Wine: A light, spicy red from Provence such as Bandol or Châteauneuf-du-Pape or a Chianti.

Chicken Jambalaya
(ALTERNATE RECIPE)

SERVES 4 to 6
PREPARATION: 20 minutes
COOKING: 40 minutes

A spicy, robust chicken-and-rice stew.

2 tablespoons vegetable oil or bacon fat
1 2-pound chicken, cut up and deboned
1 cup coarsely chopped cooked ham
½ pound spicy smoked sausage, sliced
2 medium onions, coarsely chopped
1 green bell pepper, stemmed, seeded, and
   coarsely chopped
3 celery stalks with leaves, finely chopped
1 teaspoon dried marjoram
1 teaspoon dried thyme
1 bay leaf
2 16-ounce cans whole tomatoes, coarsely
   chopped, with their juice
1 teaspoon Tabasco
2 cups chicken broth or water
2 cups uncooked white rice

■ Heat the oil in a large, deep skillet over medium heat. Add the chicken and brown lightly all over. Remove from the skillet and reserve.

■ Add the ham, sausage, vegetables, and herbs to the skillet and cook, stirring, until the vegetables are softened. Stir in the tomatoes and simmer 5 minutes. Add the Tabasco and broth. Bring the mixture to a boil, then add the rice and the reserved chicken. Lower the heat and simmer until the rice and chicken are tender, about 30 minutes.

Suggested Wine: An earthy white such as a Rhône or a California Syrah.

"Noah's Ark. Built in 2448 B.C. Gopher wood, pitched within and without. Length, three hundred cubits; width, 50 cubits; height, 30 cubits. Three decks. Cattle carrier. Owner: Noah and Sons. Last reported stranded near Mount Ararat."
Entry in the New York files of the Atlantic Mutual Insurance Co., which has one of the world's largest marine disasters archives

Garlic Bread

(ALTERNATE RECIPE)

MAKES 1 loaf
PREPARATION: 15 minutes
COOKING: 20 minutes

Redolent of garlic and herbs, lavished with olive oil, this aromatic bread brings happiness to a boat—provided everyone has his sea legs.

2 to 3 garlic cloves, pressed or minced
¼ cup chopped fresh parsley
Fresh or dried oregano, marjoram, or rosemary (optional)
6 tablespoons olive oil or unsalted butter
Salt
Freshly ground pepper
1 1-pound loaf French or Italian bread

■ Preheat oven to 375°F.

■ Make a paste of the garlic, herbs, and butter, and season to taste with salt and pepper. Cut the bread into ¾-inch-thick slices, leaving them attached at the bottom. Spread a thin layer of the paste on the face of each slice. Wrap the loaf in foil, leaving the top partially opened.

■ Bake the bread until the top is crusty and brown, about 20 minutes.

Variation: Mix 2 to 3 minced garlic cloves with ¼ cup olive oil and brush the mixture between the bread slices. Sprinkle grated Parmesan cheese between the slices and on top of the loaf. Wrap and bake the bread according to the directions above.

Banana Crisp

SERVES 4 to 6
PREPARATION: 10 minutes
COOKING: 20 minutes

A comforting yet sophisticated way to end a meal. Serve warm with fresh cream, yogurt, or ice cream.

4 large firm ripe bananas
1 tablespoon freshly squeezed lime or lemon juice
Grated nutmeg
1 teaspoon grated lime or orange rind (optional)
3 tablespoons brown sugar

Topping
½ cup all-purpose flour, or a mixture of flour and oatmeal
¼ cup brown sugar
¼ cup (½ stick) butter

■ Preheat the oven to 400°F. Butter a 9-inch pie pan or shallow baking dish.

■ Peel the bananas and slice them on the diagonal in ¼-inch ovals. Arrange the slices in a single overlapping layer and sprinkle with lime juice, nutmeg, lime rind, and sugar.

■ To make the topping, combine the flour, sugar, and butter in a bowl. With your fingertips, blend the ingredients until the mixture resembles coarse crumbs. Sprinkle evenly over the bananas.

■ Bake the bananas until the juices are bubbly and the topping is crisp and brown, about 20 minutes.

OVERHEARD

■

Eminently practical and unpretentious, Maine natives are known for speaking their minds. Here are a couple of our favorite quips:

· In North Haven, two fishermen watched calmly as a summer resident—a distinguished Harvard professor—nearly hit several anchored yachts while sailing a small boat in the thoroughfare. "Professor *knows* an awful lot," said one to the other, "but he don't realize nothin'."

· In Seal Harbor, a gardener for the Rockefellers commented on the family's extensive abstract art collection. "A-yup," he chuckled, sipping coffee at a local diner, "they like everything that don't look like anything."

Nantucket Night

RIGHT: A delicious blueberry-almond crisp.

OPPOSITE: A romantic and inviting buffet supper topside.

Thirty miles off the eastern reaches of Cape Cod lies Nantucket, from the Algonquian word *Nanticut,* which means "the faraway land." Settled by the English in 1641, the island is steeped in history, evident today from the magnificent whaling captains' mansions and snug seamen's cottages along the cobbled streets in town. The rest of the island is a romantic landscape of kettle ponds, untamed moors, fields of heather, and sandy bluffs overlooking the Atlantic Ocean.

Those who love the island debate which is her best season. Winter holidays take on a Dickensian mood when islanders decorate wooden doors and leaded-glass windows with fragrant wreaths of evergreens and bayberries. With spring comes clear blue skies, warm sea breezes, and sunny daffodils. Summer is the prime time for beachcombers, bikers, and kite flyers to enjoy the ocean beaches and tiny outer-island settlements. But perhaps the sweetest season is fall, when the crowds are gone and one has the sense of owning "the little gray lady of the sea" again. September and October also offer some of the best sailing, with crisp breezes filling the sails of boats on Nantucket Sound and the lingering warmth of a sunny day a wistful reminder that the season is soon ending.

This menu, which mixes plain Yankee fare with lively Portuguese food, is one of our fall favorites. A creamy New England clam chowder is followed by a dish made with *linguiça,* a spicy Portuguese sausage. The dinner concludes with a juicy, sugar-crusted crisp guaranteed to take the chill out of the evening air.

NANTUCKET LORE

■

Legend has it that an ancient Nantucket skipper could tell his schooner's position in the foggiest weather by tasting what the sounding lead brought up. One day his crew decided to put him to the test. They greased the lead, dunked it into a dirt bed of parsnips on board, and took it to the skipper. Upon sampling it:

The skipper stormed and tore his hair,
Thrust on his boots, and roared to Marden,
"Nantucket's sunk, and here we are
Right over old Marm Hackett's garden!"

"Mainiac's" Clam Chowder

SERVES 4 to 6
PREPARATION: 15 minutes
COOKING: 30 minutes

We first made this chowder years ago on a blustery October day while setting sail from northern Maine to Nantucket. We chatted in the cockpit, peeling potatoes and flinging clamshells overboard, our cheeks rosy from the wind. Just after dark our idyll ended abruptly when we steamed onto Duxbury Beach under full sail. In those terrible moments, as our beautiful sloop crashed in the pounding surf, the chowder simmered away, swinging wildly on the trusty Shipmate without spilling a drop. After realizing we were spending the night high and dry on the beach, we settled in and devoured the chowder, calming our nerves with a bottle of Jim Beam.

4 dozen hard-shell clams, scrubbed, or 1
  quart shucked cooked clams with their
  broth
¼ pound salt pork or 6 slices bacon
1 onion, coarsely chopped
6 medium potatoes, peeled and cut into
  ½-inch cubes
2 cups milk
2 cups half-and-half or evaporated milk
6 tablespoons (¾ stick) unsalted butter
Salt
Freshly ground pepper

■ Place the hard-shell clams in a large pot with 1 cup water, cover, bring to a boil, and cook until the shells open, about 10 minutes. Allow to cool, then shuck the clams and reserve. Pour off and reserve the broth, taking care not to disturb any sediment in the bottom of the pan.

■ Cook the salt pork in a large saucepan over medium heat until the fat runs. Add the onion and cook, stirring, until it is tender. Pour off half the fat.

■ Add the potatoes to the pan and stir well. Add the clam broth and water to just cover the potatoes. Simmer until the potatoes are tender.

■ Add the milk and half-and-half and bring to a simmer. Add the clams and butter and simmer for a few minutes, until the clams heat through and the butter melts. (Do not boil or the clams will be tough.) Season to taste with salt and pepper.

Ernestina's Fish Chowder
(ALTERNATE RECIPE)

SERVES 6 to 8
PREPARATION: 30 minutes
COOKING: 40 minutes

During an Operation Sail celebration in New York Harbor, Elizabeth made this chowder on a coal-burning stove for one hundred guests aboard the *Ernestina*, a restored Cape Verdian fishing schooner from New Bedford, Massachusetts.

5 carrots, peeled and sliced ½ inch thick
3 celery stalks, sliced ½ inch thick
2 pounds potatoes (6 to 8 medium
  potatoes), peeled and cut into 1-inch
  chunks
4 medium onions, peeled and thinly sliced
2 bay leaves
3 whole cloves
1 tablespoon dried dill
2 to 3 teaspoons salt
1 teaspoon freshly ground pepper
4 cups water
2 cups white wine
4 pounds boneless, skinless firm white fish
  (cod, halibut, etc.), cut into 2-inch
  pieces
2 cups heavy cream or evaporated milk
½ cup all-purpose flour
4 tablespoons (½ stick) unsalted butter

■ Put the vegetables in a large kettle. Add the bay leaves and cloves (tied in a cheesecloth bag, if desired), dill, salt, pepper, and water. Bring to a boil over high heat. Lower the heat and simmer until the vegetables are barely tender, about 20 minutes. Remove the bay leaves and cloves.

- Add the wine and fish and stir gently to combine ingredients. Turn off the heat, cover the pot, and let stand for 10 minutes.

- Stir the cream into the flour gradually, mixing until smooth. Gently stir the mixture into the kettle, keeping the fish intact. Return the chowder to the heat and simmer gently until thickened, about 3 to 4 minutes. Add the butter. Season with additional salt and pepper if desired. Serve immediately.

Suggested Wine: A crisp, fragrant white such as a California Semillon or a white Bordeaux.

Linguiça with Peppers

SERVES 6
PREPARATION: 15 minutes
COOKING: 30 minutes

Linguiça can be either sweet or spiked with hot peppers, but it is always orangered from the paprika that distinguishes this savory sausage.

1½ to 2 pounds sweet or hot linguiça
4 to 6 tablespoons water or white wine
3 or 4 tablespoons olive oil
1 large onion, halved and cut into
  ⅛-inch slices
4 green or red bell peppers, or a mixture,
  stemmed, seeded, and sliced
2 garlic cloves, finely chopped
½ teaspoon dried oregano
Salt
Freshly ground pepper
2 to 3 teaspoons red wine vinegar

- Coil the sausage in a skillet and add the water. Cook over medium heat until the liquid evaporates and the sausage begins to sizzle. Continue to cook, turning the sausage once, until it is browned all over. Remove the sausage and set aside. When the sausage is cool enough to handle, cut it into ½-inch slices.

- Pour the fat from the pan and add the olive oil. Add the onion, peppers, garlic, and oregano and cook, stirring, until the peppers are tender, about 10 minutes. Return the sausage to the pan and simmer until heated through. Season with salt, pepper, and vinegar.

Suggested Wine: An earthy, fruity red such as Zinfandel.

Blueberry Crisp

PREPARATION: 15 minutes
COOKING: 30 to 40 minutes

4 cups fresh blueberries
⅓ cup granulated sugar
¼ teaspoon grated lemon zest (optional)

Topping
¾ cup all-purpose flour
¼ cup rolled oats
⅓ cup packed brown sugar
¼ teaspoon cinnamon
5 tablespoons unsalted butter
½ cup lightly toasted sliced almonds

- Preheat the oven to 375°F. Lightly butter a 1-quart baking dish. Mix the blueberries, sugar, and lemon zest in the baking dish and spread in an even layer.

- Make the topping: mix the flour, oats, brown sugar, and cinnamon in a bowl. Cut the butter into small pieces and toss with the dry ingredients. With your fingertips, work in the butter until the mixture is crumbly. Add the almonds. Sprinkle the topping evenly over the berries. Bake for 30 to 40 minutes, until the top is golden brown and the juices are bubbling. Serve warm.

IBERIAN INFLUENCE
■

Southeastern Massachusetts is home to many Portuguese whose ancestors emigrated on fishing schooners from the Azores and Cape Verde Islands. Their culinary heritage adds a wonderful twist to the local cuisine with delicacies such as *linguiça*, kale soup, and sweet Portuguese bread. For lunch, many people like to split the *linguiça* in half lengthwise, put it on the grill, then stuff the sizzling, juicy sausage into a fresh Portuguese roll.

ON THE BEACH

New England Clambake

To New Englanders, the clambake is as cherished and steeped in tradition as Boston's Old North Church and Paul Revere's ride. These are huge, festive affairs, held on the beach in the summertime, involving many friends and family to dig a hole in the sand, gather rocks and firewood, and prepare mounds of lobster, soft-shell clams, spicy sausage, and milky sweet corn-on-the-cob for the pit. The event stretches through the hot afternoon into the cool evening as the rich, smoky aroma of smoldering seaweed and seafood mingles with the sharp salt air.

Although clambakes are delectable anywhere, we find them irresistible while cruising along the Maine coast, where one can easily find a protected beach, not to mention the best lobster in the world. While under sail in the morning, you might approach a friendly lobsterman hauling pots and ask to buy fresh lobster. Then after finding a beach, send several crew members ashore to dig for clams while others wander up the lane for fresh corn at a farmer's market. In mid-July and August, when wild raspberries and blueberries are in season, send teenagers and children inland with baskets to forage for dessert.

When everyone meets back at the beach, serve casual hors d'oeuvres that people can snack on during the after-noon. With plenty of iced tea, soft drinks, and beer on hand, you might play volleyball, Frisbee, or other beach games while waiting to open the bake. To eat by seven, start digging the pit no later than noon.

Preparing the Bake

While others are preparing the food, corral the heartiest mates and set them to digging the pit, gathering plenty of wet seaweed, and putting together the bake as follows:

■ Dig a round hole 2 feet deep and 4 feet wide in the sand, close to the high-water mark.

■ Line the bottom and sides of the pit with stones the size of footballs. (Stones that haven't previously been used for a bake will retain heat better.)

■ Start a charcoal fire in the bottom of the pit and feed it with hardwood.

■ When the fire is blazing and the wood has burned down, place more stones on the fire, taking care not to smother it. Soak the canvas in seawater.

■ Build a fire on top of the second layer of rocks and allow the wood to burn down. You are now ready to begin cooking. (If you do not yet want to begin the bake, maintain the fire by building another fire on top of the embers.)

Spiced Almonds

MAKES about 4 cups
PREPARATION: 15 minutes
COOKING: 20 minutes

A tasty snack to munch on while preparing the bake.

2 egg whites
1 pound whole almonds (about 4 cups)
½ teaspoon salt
1 tablespoon sugar
1 tablespoon ground cumin
2 teaspoons ground cinnamon
½ teaspoon cayenne (ground red) pepper

■ Heat the oven to 350°F.

■ Beat the egg whites with a fork in a mixing bowl until slightly frothy. Add the nuts and mix well to coat. Drain the nuts in a sieve to remove the excess egg white and return to the mixing bowl. Add the salt, sugar, and spices and toss well.

■ Spread the nuts on a lightly oiled baking sheet. Bake the nuts about 20 minutes, stirring occasionally with a wooden spoon to separate them, until they are crisp and golden. Turn off the oven and leave the nuts inside for about 30 minutes. Store in an airtight container.

Taco Pie

SERVES 10
PREPARATION: 30 minutes

This gloriously vulgar concoction has been devoured every time we've made it. Serve with plenty of crisp tortilla chips.

1 16-ounce can refried beans
1 8-ounce jar chunky tomato salsa
1 cup (8 ounces) sour cream
2 cups Guacamole (recipe follows)
1½ cups shredded Monterey Jack or Cheddar cheese
1 to 2 cups shredded lettuce
2 to 3 ripe tomatoes, seeded and chopped

3 or 4 scallions including green tops, finely sliced crosswise
½ cup sliced black olives
Tortilla chips

■ Combine the beans and salsa in a 9-inch pie plate or similar shallow dish. Mix well and spread across the bottom of the pie plate in an even layer. Stir the sour cream until smooth and spread it in an even layer over the beans. Follow with a layer of Guacamole. Sprinkle the cheese on top.

■ Arrange the lettuce, tomatoes, scallions, and olives decoratively over the cheese, either in alternating bands or in concentric circles.

■ Chill the Taco Pie until ready to serve and serve with tortilla chips.

Guacamole

MAKES ABOUT 2 cups
PREPARATION: 10 minutes

This delicate green sauce should be covered as soon as it is prepared, or it will discolor and lose its fresh taste. If fresh cilantro is available, add a few tablespoons of roughly chopped leaves.

2 medium ripe avocados (see Note)
1 fresh or canned chile, finely chopped, or Tabasco to taste
2 or 3 scallions, finely chopped, or ¼ cup finely chopped onion
Salt
1 to 2 tablespoons freshly squeezed lime juice or lemon juice

■ Cut the avocados in half and remove the pits. Scoop the avocado flesh from the skins and place in a small mixing bowl. Add the remaining ingredients and mash to a coarse puree with a fork.

Note: Haas avocados with their nubbly black skins and rich, buttery flesh are far superior to the larger, green smooth-skinned Florida avocados, which are often watery and insipid.

- Shovel, boathook, iron rake
- Bucket
- Cheesecloth
- Large mesh bag, such as a fifty-pound onion bag
- Canvas (at least five feet square when doubled over), soaked in seawater
- Wire mesh tacked onto a wooden frame to serve as a tray for the lobster, corn, and *linguiça*

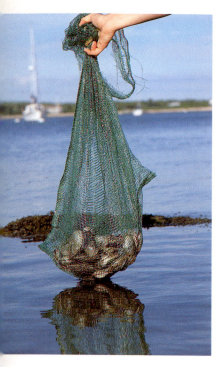

We used an onion bag to rinse the clams in sea water.

Clambake

SERVES 6
PREPARATION: 30 minutes, excluding the pit
COOKING: 1½ hours

6 live lobsters, about 1½ pounds each
6 pounds soft-shell clams
12 ears fresh sweet corn
6 large white boiling potatoes
6 large yellow sweet potatoes
6 medium red, yellow, or white onions
2 or 3 pound length of linguiça, kielbasa, or other spicy sausage
Melted unsalted butter (about ¾ pound or 3 sticks)

■ Keep lobsters alive and cool under a blanket of seaweed in the shade.

■ Soak the clams in sea water for several hours, then pour them into a mesh bag large enough to hold clams in a flat layer. Tie the bag.

■ If desired, prepare the corn by carefully peeling back the leaves from the ears one by one, keeping them attached; then strip away the silk. Smooth the leaves back over the ears and secure with string. Soak the corn in a bucket of seawater.

■ Scrub the potatoes and place them in a loose cheesecloth sling.

■ Remove the loose skins from the onions, leaving the innermost layer of skin intact. Cut an **X** in the root end of each onion with a sharp knife.

■ Wrap the sausage in a cheesecloth sling.

■ Take the ingredients to the pit, and working quickly, rake away the embers and throw a 6-inch layer of wet seaweed over the rocks. (Be generous with the seaweed.) Place the potatoes and onions on top. Cover with more wet seaweed. Add the lobster, corn, and sausage (in a wire mesh tray, if you have one). Cover with wet seaweed. Place the clams on top and cover with a final layer of wet seaweed.

■ Cover the mound with the soaked

ON THE BEACH

"When one has tasted watermelons one knows what angels eat."

Mark Twain

canvas and seal the edges with sand so the steam can't escape. Cook for 1½ hours, occasionally dousing the canvas with water.

■ When it is time to open the bake, carefully lift the corner of the canvas with an oar or boathook and peel it back, taking care to keep the sand away from the food. Rake away the seaweed, lifting out the bag of clams and the cheesecloth sling of sausage with a boathook. If you are using a frame, lift it from the pit and remove the lobsters and corn. Rake back the final layer of seaweed and remove the slings of potatoes and onions.

■ Serve the food immediately with melted butter. For dessert, offer fresh berries or watermelon cut into wedges. A few Thermoses of coffee may be very welcome after the meal, along with a good Cognac or rum to sip by the fire as the evening winds down.

Suggested Wine: A California Chardonnay.

Creamy Coleslaw

SERVES 4 to 6
PREPARATION: 20 minutes

For extra crispness, soak the shredded cabbage in cold water for 30 minutes and drain thoroughly before tossing with the dressing.

3 to 4 tablespoons finely chopped onion
½ cup mayonnaise
½ cup sour cream
2 to 3 tablespoons white wine or cider vinegar
1 tablespoon Dijon mustard
1 teaspoon dill seed
1 teaspoon Worcestershire sauce
Freshly ground pepper
4 cups packed finely shredded green cabbage

■ Whisk together all the ingredients except the cabbage in a large mixing bowl and season to taste with pepper. Add the cabbage and toss thoroughly.

■ Cover the salad and chill for at least 1 hour before serving. Toss lightly and adjust seasoning just before serving.

Lake Breakfast

Last summer we had the rare pleasure of fishing at dawn on a pristine mountain lake. At four in the morning, with pale light filtering through the portholes, we loaded the fishing tackle and breakfast supplies into the dinghy. The wooden oars creaked and groaned in the silence as we rowed across the dark lake to a secluded, spruce-fringed cove.

While we were casting, light broke across the slate-blue mountains as an eerie mist spiraled from the cool lake surface. A deer appeared at water's edge for a morning drink, then vanished. We sat silently in the dinghy, observing the wildlife, anticipating the insistent tug on the line that would mean breakfast.

Three hours later, with a full string of trout trailing behind the stern, we rowed to a nearby island—actually a clump of rocks and some scrubby trees. It seemed like high noon with the heat of the sun warming our backs, but it was barely eight o'clock. After scouting for a suitable place to build a fire, we took a quick dip in the chilly water, then enjoyed a hearty camp breakfast.

Cowboy Coffee

- To make robust coffee the old-fashioned way, toss water, coffee, and a pinch of salt into a saucepan and quickly bring the water to a boil. Adjust the pan's position over the heat so that the coffee is barely simmering and cook for about 5 minutes.

- Remove the pan from the heat and allow the coffee to stand for 2 to 3 minutes to allow the grounds to settle. Or, add a few egg shells to help coagulate the grounds and splash in a bit of water to settle the grounds quickly.

- Pour or ladle the coffee into cups.

Panfried Trout with Bacon

SERVES 2
PREPARATION: 5 minutes
COOKING: 10 minutes

Anyone who has caught his own trout knows the keen pleasure of an early morning fishing breakfast.

Sliced bacon
2 small trout (about 12 ounces each),
    cleaned
Salt (optional)
Freshly ground pepper (optional)
All-purpose flour or cornmeal

- Prepare the grill (page 13).

- Place the bacon slices in a cold large skillet. Cook the bacon slowly until it is crisp and brown. Remove the bacon, leaving the fat in the pan.

- Sprinkle the trout inside and out with salt and pepper, if desired, and dredge them in the flour, shaking off the excess.

- Add the fish to the pan and cook for about 5 minutes on each side, turning the fish carefully with a wide spatula. Move the pan over the coals as necessary so the trout will brown evenly. The trout should be golden brown and the tails crisp. Serve immediately.

MENU

Cowboy Coffee

Panfried Trout with Bacon

Cornmeal Fritters

Potato Pancakes

■

ABOVE: We built a blazing fire on the rocks to cook the freshly caught trout.

LEFT: Colorful inexpensive enamelware is both festive and practical on a boat.

OPPOSITE: A steaming pot of cowboy coffee at dawn.

Cornmeal Fritters

MAKES ABOUT 12 fritters
PREPARATION: 5 minutes
COOKING: 10 minutes

Mix the dry ingredients ahead of time in an airtight container large enough to serve as a mixing vessel. Nestle the egg in the dry ingredients to protect it from cracking.

½ cup yellow cornmeal
2 tablespoons all-purpose flour
½ teaspoon baking powder
¼ teaspoon salt
Freshly ground pepper
1 egg
¼ to ½ cup milk or water
1 small onion, thinly sliced or finely chopped
Bacon fat or vegetable oil

■ Prepare the grill (page 13).

■ Mix the dry ingredients. Break the egg into the dry ingredients and add ¼ cup milk. Beat the mixture with a fork until just blended, adding enough milk to make a thick batter. Stir in the onion.

■ Heat bacon fat or oil in a large frying pan. Drop tablespoonfuls of the batter into the frying pan and cook until golden brown on both sides. Drain on paper towels or a paper bag. Serve immediately.

Potato Pancakes

SERVES 4 to 6
PREPARATION: 10 minutes
COOKING: 15 minutes

Delicious and surprisingly easy.

4 to 5 medium potatoes
2 eggs
3 to 4 tablespoons grated or finely chopped onion
2 to 3 tablespoons all-purpose flour
Salt
Freshly ground pepper
¼ teaspoon baking powder (optional)
Vegetable oil, bacon fat, or a mixture of butter and vegetable oil

■ Prepare the grill (page 13).

■ Grate the potatoes coarsely into a bowl and drain off as much liquid as possible.

■ Add the eggs, onion, and flour to the potatoes and mix well. Add salt and pepper to taste. (If using baking powder, stir it into the mixture thoroughly just before frying.)

■ Heat a large, heavy skillet over medium heat. Add enough oil to lightly coat the bottom of the pan. When oil is hot, drop the batter by tablespoonfuls into the skillet. Press each pancake flat with a spatula. Cook the pancakes, turning once, until they are crisp and golden brown. Serve at once.

Sunday on the Beach

Although we grew up in different latitudes, we have similar memories of childhood weekends on the water. Beach days were a festive commotion of friends and relatives dragging an array of coolers, hampers, beach bags, inner tubes, and towels across the sand. Then, while the kids looked for horseshoe crabs or shells, the adults unpacked lavish picnics that included cold chicken sandwiches, ribs for the barbecue, raw vegetables, wide pans of chocolate cake, and plenty of fruit.

The picnic food here is easily assembled on board or at home, and can withstand the jostling that accompanies boat picnics. Just check that all containers are leak-proof and that the tops are firmly fastened. For all-day affairs, we also take along a Sunday paper, big cotton napkins or dish towels, and a few insulated bottles filled with freshly brewed coffee and our favorite libations.

Cheddar Corn Bread

SERVES 6 to 8
PREPARATION: 15 minutes
COOKING: 40 minutes

½ cup vegetable oil
3 eggs
1 cup sour cream, buttermilk, or yogurt
1 16-ounce can cream-style corn
2 cups yellow cornmeal
2 teaspoons baking powder
1 teaspoon salt
1 cup grated Cheddar cheese

■ Preheat the oven to 350°F. Brush 1 tablespoon oil into a 9-inch-square baking pan or a 10-inch cast-iron skillet. If using the skillet, heat it in the oven for 10 minutes before brushing it with the oil to give the bread a crisp crust.

■ Whisk the remaining oil and the eggs in a mixing bowl. Stir in the sour cream and corn.

■ Mix the cornmeal, baking powder, and salt, then add it to the egg mixture, and stir until the dry ingredients are moistened. Fold in ½ cup of the cheese, reserving the remaining ½ cup. Pour the batter into the prepared pan and sprinkle the reserved cheese on top.

■ Bake until the bread is risen, browned, and firm to the touch, about 40 minutes. Allow to cool 10 minutes before cutting.

Variation: Embellished with nuggets of spicy sausage and vegetables, the following version is a meal in itself.

Preheat the oven to 350°F. and assemble the ingredients for the corn bread batter. Combine 1 medium finely chopped onion, 1 or 2 seeded and chopped jalapeño peppers, 1 small seeded and chopped green bell pepper, and 4 ounces chopped spicy sausage such as chorizo in a skillet and cook over moderate heat, stirring occasionally, until the vegetables are tender and the sausage is cooked. Pour off the excess fat and let the mixture cool. Prepare the corn bread batter and fold in the sausage mixture. Pour the batter into the prepared pan and bake until risen, browned, and firm to the touch, about 45 minutes.

MENU

Cheddar Corn Bread

Pepper, Ham, and Potato Frittata

Bull Shots

Pineapple Wedges or Fresh Fruit Salad

■

Sunday boating pleasures.

LEFT: A casual Sunday brunch on the beach includes a savory frittata, cheddar corn bread, fresh pineapple, and a big pitcher of chilled bull shots.

BELOW: A pan of pepper, ham, and potato frittata.

Pepper, Ham, and Potato Frittata

SERVES 6
PREPARATION: 20 minutes
COOKING: 30 minutes

This fat, juicy omelet is traditional picnic fare in Spain and Portugal. You can make it on the boat and take it ashore in the skillet. Or, if your picnic gets rained out, cut the frittata into squares, simmer it in tomato sauce, and serve with freshly grated Parmesan cheese.

4 or 5 medium red potatoes, thinly sliced
½ cup olive oil, vegetable oil, or a mixture
1 medium onion, thinly sliced
1 sweet red bell pepper, stemmed, seeded, and thinly sliced
¼ pound thinly sliced ham or Canadian bacon
Salt
8 eggs
Freshly ground pepper

■ Preheat the oven to 350°F.

■ Pat the potatoes dry to remove the excess moisture.

■ Heat the oil in a heavy, deep 12-inch skillet over medium heat. Add alternating layers of potatoes and onion, pepper and ham, salting each lightly. Cover the pan and cook gently for about 20 minutes, shaking the pan occasionally and lifting the potatoes carefully to prevent sticking, until the vegetables are tender. Pour off and reserve the excess oil for later use.

■ Beat the eggs with a whisk in a large bowl until foamy. Add the vegetable mixture and stir gently. Season to taste with pepper.

■ Wipe the skillet clean and return it to the heat. Add 2 tablespoons of the reserved oil. Heat until sizzling and add the egg mixture. Spread the mixture in the pan. Reduce the heat to moderate and cook, shaking the pan occasionally, until the eggs are set on the bottom and still slightly liquid on top. Cook in the oven for about 10 minutes, until eggs are set (see Note).

■ Serve the frittata warm or at room temperature, cut into wedges. Do not refrigerate.

Note: If you don't have an oven, cook the mixture a little longer until the eggs are almost set. Slide a spatula underneath the frittata to make sure it is not sticking, then invert it onto a plate. Add a little oil to the pan and slide the frittata back into the skillet to brown the other side.

Variation: Try this dish with other vegetables such as eggplant, zucchini, or asparagus.

Carrot Pecan Bread

(ALTERNATE RECIPE)

MAKES one 9 x 5-inch loaf
PREPARATION: 20 minutes
COOKING: 40 minutes

This fragrant, carrot-flecked bread goes well with cream cheese, marmalade, and sliced ham or smoked turkey.

1 cup all-purpose flour
1 cup whole wheat flour
2 teaspoons baking powder
½ teaspoon baking soda
¼ teaspoon salt
1 teaspoon cinnamon
2 eggs
½ cup sour cream, plain yogurt, or milk
¼ cup orange juice
½ cup maple syrup or honey
⅓ cup vegetable oil or melted unsalted butter
1 teaspoon vanilla extract
1 cup grated carrots (about 3 medium carrots), packed
½ cup coarsely broken pecans or walnuts
½ cup snipped dates (about 6 large dates) or raisins

■ Preheat the oven to 350°F. Lightly butter a 9 x 5-inch loaf pan (see Note).

■ Combine the dry ingredients in a bowl and blend with a whisk. In a separate bowl, combine the eggs, sour cream, and orange juice and blend with a whisk. Stir in the syrup, oil, and vanilla.

■ Add the liquid ingredients to the flour mixture and stir just until the dry ingredients are moistened. Fold in the carrots, nuts, and dates. Turn the batter into the prepared pan.

■ Bake until the loaf is browned and a toothpick inserted in the center comes out clean, about 40 minutes.

Note: For muffins, fill 12 buttered or paper-lined muffin cups ⅔ full and bake for about 20 minutes.

Bull Shots

MAKES 1 drink

Serve this spicy drink chilled on a hot summer afternoon or piping hot on a crisp fall night.

¼ cup beef broth
½ cup tomato juice or V-8 juice
Freshly ground pepper
Worcestershire sauce
1 teaspoon prepared horseradish
Tabasco
1 shot vodka (optional)
Lemon slice or celery (garnish)

■ Combine the broth and tomato juice and season with pepper, Worcestershire sauce, horseradish, and Tabasco. Pour the mixture into a Thermos. If you are serving the Bull Shot cold, fill an additional Thermos with ice and take it along to add ice to the drink. To serve hot, heat to just under a boil and keep hot in a Thermos.

■ At the last minute, add a shot of vodka, and garnish with a thin slice of lemon.

Note: To make a pitcher of Bull Shots, use 2 10-ounce cans beef broth, 1 48-ounce can tomato juice, 2 to 3 tablespoons horseradish, and season to taste with the remaining ingredients.

Sangrita

(ALTERNATE RECIPE)

SERVES 4
PREPARATION: 10 minutes

A tangy tomato drink traditionally served with shots of tequila.

3 cups tomato juice or V-8 juice
¾ cup freshly squeezed orange juice
¼ cup freshly squeezed lime juice (about 3 limes)
1 small onion, grated
1 teaspoon Tabasco
Salt

■ Combine the ingredients in a pitcher and stir well. Add salt to taste. Strain, if desired, and pour the Sangrita into tall glasses filled with ice.

FRESH FRUIT SALAD
■

Because they are easy to make, fruit salads are a favorite on boats. Use complementary colors and flavors and avoid jumbling the salad with too many fruits (we rarely use more than five). Add cantaloupes, bananas, raspberries, or other soft berries at the last moment to prevent them from becoming soggy. Sweeten salads lightly with sugar, a thread of honey, your favorite liqueur, or a splash of orange juice. Some popular combinations:

· Cantaloupe, honeydew, and blueberries tossed with lime juice and fresh mint (see Note).

· Strawberries, oranges, and blueberries.

· Grapefruit and oranges tossed with fresh mint (see Note) and honey and garnished with cherries or purple grapes.

· Pineapple and strawberries sprinkled with Cointreau or Triple Sec.

· Peaches, plums, and blueberries.

Note: If you lack fresh mint, revive a teaspoon of dried mint by steeping it for 10 minutes in a tablespoon of white wine, lemon juice, or lime juice.

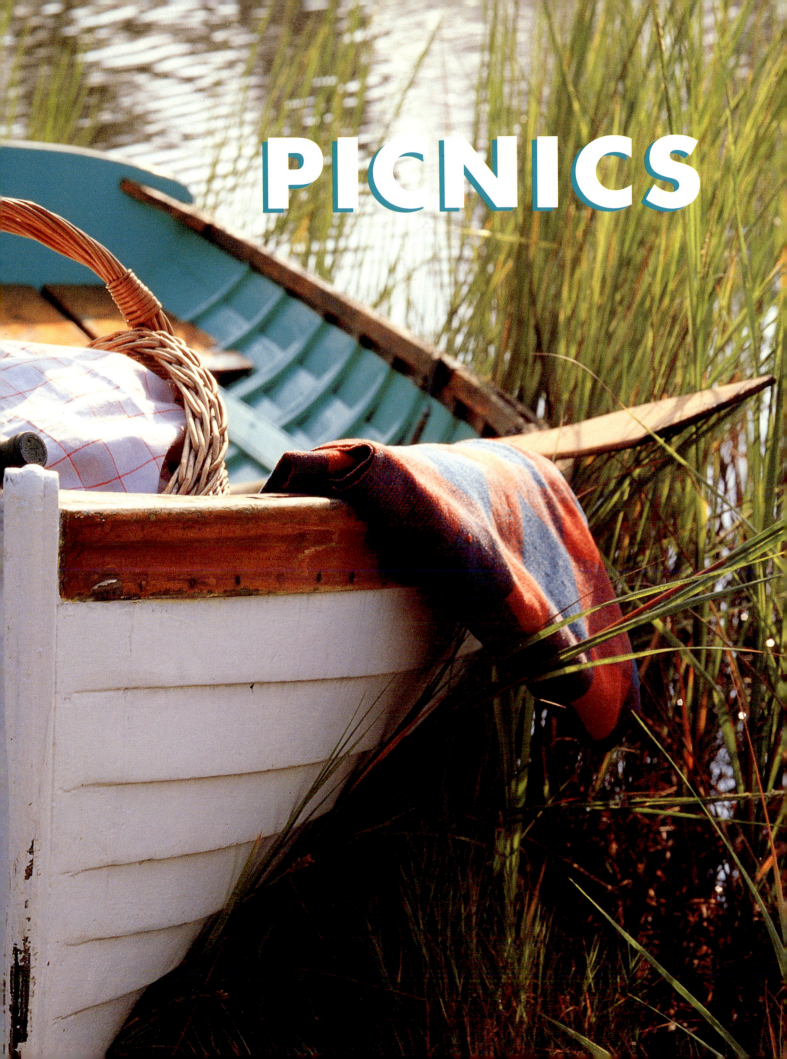

PICNICS

Up a Creek

All along the craggy coast of southeastern Massachusetts, winding creeks snake inland past tangled rose canes, rustling eelgrass, and fragrant pine groves. These mysterious inlets, sheltered and remote, beckon to be explored. Songbirds, deer, and an occasional red fox may be seen at river bends, while grassy knolls offer romantic havens for late afternoon picnics.

Once the anchor is set, we're fond of packing a picnic for a leisurely outing up one of these creeks. Although yachting is essentially a casual sport, an elegant mood can be created by bringing along good china, crystal glasses, and cloth linens, not to mention an antique telescope for bird-watching. The blanket (and later the galley table) can be decorated with a spray of powder blue chicory, small white asters, and seaside goldenrod gathered along the way.

Roast Pork and Orange Salad

SERVES 2 to 4
PREPARATION: 20 minutes

Cold roast pork is delicious in this tangy, bright salad.

1 pound cold roasted or grilled pork tenderloin, thinly sliced
2 or 3 scallions (white and green parts), thinly sliced
1 red bell pepper, stem and seeds removed, thinly sliced

Dressing
1 tablespoon soy sauce
1 teaspoon finely chopped fresh ginger root
1 garlic clove, finely chopped
1 teaspoon Dijon mustard
1 teaspoon sugar
2 tablespoons white wine or cider vinegar
⅓ cup vegetable oil
3 navel oranges

■ Put the pork in a mixing bowl with the scallions and pepper slices. Combine the dressing ingredients in a container with a tight-fitting lid, shake vigorously, and pour over the meat. Toss lightly and set aside to marinate 10 minutes.

■ With a small, sharp knife, cut the peel from the oranges, taking care to remove the white pith. Cut the oranges in half lengthwise, then crosswise into ⅛-inch-thick half-moons. Arrange the pork, vegetables, and oranges in overlapping rows in a container. Top with the remaining dressing.

Note: Grilled beef, chicken, or lamb can be substituted for the pork.

Suggested Wine: A California Chenin Blanc or a Beaujolais.

Chinese Chicken Salad
(ALTERNATE RECIPE)

SERVES 4 to 6
PREPARATION: 20 minutes
COOKING: 20 minutes

Ever since we first made this, crews have clamored for more.

4 chicken breast halves
2 whole scallions, trimmed
2 thin slices fresh ginger root
1 teaspoon salt
4 to 6 scallions, thinly sliced
1 cup canned water chestnuts, drained
    and thinly sliced.

Dressing
1 tablespoon finely chopped fresh ginger
    root
1 teaspoon dry mustard
1 tablespoon brown sugar
¼ cup cider or rice wine vinegar
½ cup vegetable oil
2 tablespoons sesame oil
Freshly ground pepper
Salt to taste

Shredded Romaine lettuce or cabbage
Sesame seeds (optional)

■ Put the chicken breasts in a large skillet with the whole scallions and ginger. Add water to barely cover the chicken and bring to a boil over high heat. Add the salt and lower the heat. Simmer, partially covered, for about 20 minutes, or until chicken is tender (see Note). Remove the skillet from the heat and let the chicken cool in the broth.

■ Remove the meat from the chicken breasts, discarding the skin and bones. With your fingers, tear the meat into shreds and toss with the sliced scallions and water chestnuts.

■ Combine the dressing ingredients in a container with a tight-fitting lid and shake vigorously.

■ Pour half the dressing onto the chicken and toss lightly. Spoon the salad onto a bed of shredded lettuce and drizzle with the remaining dressing. Sprinkle with sesame seeds, if desired.

Variation: For a delicious garnish, remove the skin from the chicken breasts before poaching, marinate in a little soy sauce, and fry until crisp. Slice finely and scatter over the salad.

Suggested Wine: A crisp dry white such as Rioja.

Fusilli with Peanut Sauce

SERVES 3 to 4
PREPARATION: 15 minutes
COOKING: 10 minutes

With its creamy, aromatic sau. noodle salad with a Chinese accent . itively addictive.

½ pound fusilli or corkscrew pasta

Peanut Sauce
4 to 5 tablespoons peanut butter (see
    Note)
2 teaspoons brown or granulated sugar
    (see Note)
2 garlic cloves, peeled and finely chopped
2 teaspoons finely chopped fresh ginger
    root
2 tablespoons vegetable oil
2 tablespoons soy sauce
1 tablespoon cider vinegar
4 to 5 tablespoons boiling water (from
    cooking the fusilli)
1 tablespoon sesame oil

Garnish
Sesame seeds

■ Bring a large pot of salted water to a boil. Cook the fusilli until just tender, about 10 minutes.

■ While the fusilli cooks, combine all the sauce ingredients except the water in a small mixing bowl. With a whisk, slowly incorporate the liquid ingredients into the peanut butter, making a stiff paste. Whisk in the hot water by the tablespoonful, until the sauce has the consistency of heavy cream.

■ Drain the fusilli, shaking off the excess water. Add the noodles to the sauce, sprinkle with the sesame oil, and toss well. Sprinkle sesame seeds over the top.

■ Serve within 4 hours. Do not refrigerate or the noodles will become stiff and sticky.

Note: If using commerically processed peanut butter, omit the sugar from the sauce, and add it later, if necessary, after tasting.

a.
mo.
in th.
langua.
    Henry,
        by Edi.

ABOVE: **Roast pork and orange salad, and noodles with creamy peanut sauce are delightful picnic fare. O**PPOSITE: **A private and romantic setting for lunch.**

Sunny Day-Sail Picnic

Jennifer spent several summers sailing with her family on the deep waters of Casco Bay when she was a young child in southern Maine. Setting out from Falmouth Foreside in a little Beetle Swan, they would tack by the long, rocky peninsulas and wooded inner islands, picking out the eccentric names on the chart. Goose Island. Jewell Island. West Brown Cow. Sometimes they'd go ashore, startling the crows off the seaweed, to collect shells and look for osprey nests. But mostly they'd sail by, savoring the scenery and puffy breezes that filled their sail. Jennifer's mother would pack a hamper of food, and when the sun was high they'd have a picnic in the cockpit. These simple lunches under sail were some of Jennifer's childhood favorites.

The following day-sail picnic can be put together easily on a small boat. Taking advantage of produce from summer gardens—fat, juicy tomatoes; fragrant Italian basil; small, crisp cucumbers—we've included mostly uncooked foods that can be assembled in minutes for picnics ashore or on the doghouse. Only the brownies and hard-boiled eggs need to be made ahead.

Tomato and Mozzarella Sandwiches on Italian Bread

SERVES 4
PREPARATION: 15 minutes plus 1 hour marinating

> *1 pound fresh mozzarella cheese, thinly sliced, or substitute Brie, goat cheese, Havarti, or other soft cheese*
> *4 to 6 tablespoons Garlic Vinaigrette (recipe follows)*
> *Freshly ground pepper*
> *Crushed red pepper (optional)*
> *1-pound loaf long, thin Italian or French bread*
> *2 or 3 firm ripe red tomatoes*
> *Lettuce, arugula, or basil leaves, washed and dried*

■ Layer the sliced cheese in a bowl with 2 or 3 tablespoons vinaigrette and season with pepper and crushed red pepper.

■ Slice the loaf of bread lengthwise, without cutting through, so that it is hinged. Pull out the soft inner crumbs from the loaf, making a slight hollow, and brush the insides generously with the vinaigrette.

■ Slice the tomatoes into ⅛-inch-thick rounds. Place overlapping slices of the tomatoes and cheese on one half of the bread, and sprinkle with a little vinaigrette. Cover with lettuce. Close the sandwich and wrap tightly in wax paper or aluminum foil. Put the sandwich under 10 pounds or so of weight for about 1 hour to distribute the flavors and moisture through the bread.

■ To serve, cut the loaf crosswise into manageable slices.

Variation: In addition to the tomatoes, layer the cheese with slices of marinated olives or artichoke hearts, anchovies, slivers of red onion, or thin slices of ham, salami, or prosciutto.

Garlic Vinaigrette

¼ cup red wine vinegar
1 to 2 large garlic cloves, peeled and lightly crushed
1 tablespoon finely chopped onion or shallot
½ teaspoon dried oregano or marjoram
2 tablespoons finely chopped fresh parsley (optional)
¾ cup olive oil

■ Combine the ingredients in a container with a tight-sealing lid and let stand for at least 2 hours. When the vinaigrette has the desired garlic flavor, fish out the garlic cloves. Shake the vinaigrette vigorously before using.

Cucumber and Yogurt Soup

SERVES 4 to 6
PREPARATION: 30 minutes

This cool, pale green soup is better than air-conditioning. Serve the soup with sandwiches and salads for lunch, or for an elegant appetizer on a summer evening, serve it in small bowls garnished with a cluster of pink shrimp, crab, or lobster.

3 or 4 cucumbers, peeled, halved, and seeded
2 tablespoons cider or rice wine vinegar
1 tablespoon sugar
1 teaspoon salt

2 cups plain yogurt
1 cup ice water
Tabasco or cayenne (ground red) pepper
2 teaspoons dried dill, or 2 tablespoons fresh dill leaves
2 to 3 scallions, finely sliced

■ Grate the cucumbers coarsely into a small bowl. Stir in the vinegar, sugar, and salt. Allow the cucumber to marinate for 15 minutes. Drain the mixture through a sieve and press firmly to remove the excess moisture.

■ Combine the cucumbers with the yogurt. Slowly stir in enough water to make a thick, creamy soup. Season to taste with salt and Tabasco. Stir in the dill and sprinkle the soup with scallions. Serve cold. (If you are taking the soup on a picnic, place it in a Thermos with a few ice cubes to chill the soup thoroughly).

Sesame Salt

MAKES 4 tablespoons
PREPARATION: 5 minutes
COOKING: 5 minutes

This traditional Japanese seasoning is delicious sprinkled over hard-boiled eggs or steamed vegetables and adds a new dimension to sesame noodles and marinades for grilled fish and meats. This recipe can be doubled or tripled if desired.

¼ cup sesame seeds
2 teaspoons salt

■ Place the sesame seeds and salt in a small saucepan over medium heat and cook, stirring constantly, until the seeds pop, turn golden, and are aromatic. Immediately pour the mixture into a small bowl to stop the cooking.

■ While the mixture is still warm, crush the seeds with a mortar and pestle; or put the seeds and salt in a heavy plastic bag and crush them with a rolling pin or the bottom of a heavy pan.

■ Store the sesame salt in an airtight container.

HARD-BOILED ADVICE
■

Anyone can boil an egg, right? Wrong. All too often eggs are overcooked, with rubbery whites and powdery yolks. For perfect hard-boiled eggs, begin by putting them in a saucepan and cover them with cold water. Bring the water to a boil over high heat. Lower the heat and cook the eggs at a bare simmer for exactly 10 minutes. Immediately pour off the hot water and plunge the eggs into a large quantity of cold water. When cool, peel the eggs if you plan to use them immediately, or store them unshelled in the refrigerator.

OPPOSITE: Aboard *Sunny-side,* a 1905 catboat, we enjoyed a simple picnic lunch.

Tomato and mozzarella sandwich served conveniently in a wax paper pocket.

Hard-boiled egg sprinkled with sesame salt.

Cotton dishtowel contains fruit and prevents it from rolling.

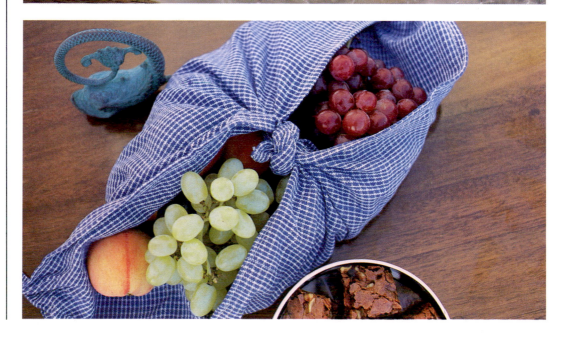

The Devil's Brownies

MAKES 20 squares
PREPARATION: 20 minutes
COOKING: 25 minutes

These outrageously rich brownies are almost a confection.

*⅓ cup dried currants or chopped dried
  apricots*
*¼ cup Scotch, rum, Cointreau, or your
  favorite liqueur*
8 tablespoons (1 stick) unsalted butter
4 ounces semisweet chocolate
1 cup firmly packed brown sugar
*1 teaspoon instant coffee, dissolved in 1
  tablespoon hot water*
3 eggs
1 teaspoon vanilla extract
¾ cup all-purpose flour
¼ teaspoon salt
1 cup walnuts, pistachios, or pecans
1 cup semisweet chocolate chips or chunks

■ Put the dried fruit and Scotch in a bowl and set aside to let the fruit absorb the liquid.

■ Preheat the oven to 350°F. For ease of cleanup, line an 8½ x 11-inch pan with overlapping sheets of foil, allowing a little overhang. Butter the foil lightly.

■ Melt the butter and 4 ounces semisweet chocolate in a saucepan large enough to double as a mixing bowl over simmering water or on a burner covered with a flame tamer. Stir the chocolate until smooth and set aside to cool slightly.

■ Beat the sugar and the coffee into the chocolate. Add the eggs one by one, beating well after each addition. Add the vanilla. Add the set aside fruit and liquid.

■ Combine the flour and salt and stir them into the chocolate mixture, until just blended. Stir in the nuts and chocolate chips.

■ Scrape the batter into the prepared pan and smooth the top. Bake the brownies until the center is set but still slightly moist, about 25 minutes. Allow the brownies to cool at least 30 minutes before cutting them into small squares.

Note: For a plain, pure chocolate brownie, omit the fruit, liqueur, coffee, nuts, and chocolate chips, and be sure not to overbake.

WHAT'S IN A NAME?

■

According to Mr. Webster, an island is "a tract of land surrounded by water and smaller than a continent." To people in the Thousand Islands in the Saint Lawrence River, any cluster of rocks with a tree qualifies.

We like islands in any shape or size, especially those with quirky names. Some of our favorites around the world are: Pumpkin Island, Pound of Tea, Butter Island, Salt Cay, Cherry Island, Cabbage Key, and, of course, the Big Apple.

To the Lighthouse

From Connecticut's sandy shoreline to the rocky harbors down east, the New England coast is rich in history and beauty. There are the snug harbors where wooden boats are as thick as quahogs and lovingly restored sea captains' houses evoke the whaling era. There are the majestic points, where weathered mansions with sweeping lawns and private docks have been in the same Brahmin families for generations. And there are the lighthouses—unadorned, solitary beacons that have dotted the New England coast for decades.

Whether we're running offshore from one big light to another or simply out for a day-sail, abandoned lighthouses are ideal places to land for lunch. Especially in the early fall, when the weather is too cool for swimming but perfect for picnicking, we like outings to these remote, windswept spots.

After securing the dinghy, we clamber over the rocks, find a protected spot to drop the picnic gear, and explore the area. We've spent hours poking in tidal pools, collecting shells, and observing wild fowl. Then we relax over a lazy lunch that stretches into the afternoon, sometimes ending with a nap in the warm September sun.

This sort of excursion calls for a menu plentiful enough to last all day. If we want to be at the boat early in the morning (and we nearly always do), we prepare food the night before, letting the chicken wings marinate while we make the corn chowder. The evening is a good time, too, to assemble odds and ends (utensils, napkins, a corkscrew) that are sometimes overlooked in the rush to get out the door. In the morning, we simply reheat the chowder, pour it into a wide-mouthed Thermos, pack it in the hamper with the other food, and go.

Artichoke Hearts and Roasted Peppers

MAKES APPROXIMATELY 3 cups
PREPARATION: 10 minutes

*2 6-ounce jars marinated artichoke
   hearts
3 large sweet red bell peppers, roasted,
   peeled and cut into strips (page 84), or
   2 6-ounce jars roasted red peppers
1 garlic clove, finely chopped
2 tablespoons red wine vinegar
1/2 teaspoon dried oregano or marjoram
3 to 4 tablespoons olive oil
2 tablespoons finely chopped fresh parsley*

■ Drain the artichoke hearts and peppers. Toss them with the remaining ingredients and store them in an airtight container. Serve at room temperature.

Variation: Make a delicious sandwich by combining Artichoke Hearts and Roasted Peppers with cheese or cold sliced meats.

M E N U

*Artichoke Hearts and
Roasted Peppers*

*Corn Chowder with
Red Potatoes*

Lemon Chicken Wings

Tabooleh

Walnut Shortbread

*Cheddar Cheese and
Apples*

■

LEFT: A hearty lunch of corn chowder, lemon chicken wings, and artichoke hearts and roasted peppers. **B**ELOW **LEFT**: Crunchy walnut shortbread with crisp red apples and a hunk of cheddar.

OPPOSITE: We spent this sunny September afternoon exploring Sheffield Island in Connecticut, where the lighthouse dates back to 1848.

Corn Chowder with Red Potatoes

SERVES 4 to 6
PREPARATION: 15 minutes
COOKING: 45 minutes

This comforting soup will warm you on a cool autumn afternoon. Crumble a few strips of crisp bacon onto the chowder before serving.

2 tablespoons unsalted butter or vegetable oil
½ cup chopped cooked ham
1 medium onion, coarsely chopped
1 celery stalk with leaves, coarsely chopped
½ teaspoon dried thyme
3 or 4 medium red potatoes, scrubbed, cut into ½-inch cubes
2 cups chicken broth or water
Salt
1 16-ounce can cream-style corn
2 cups fresh or canned evaporated milk
3 tablespoons unsalted butter, softened
3 tablespoons all-purpose flour
Freshly ground pepper
Chopped fresh parsley

■ Melt the butter over medium heat. Add the ham, onion, and celery and sauté until the vegetables are tender, about 10 minutes. Add the thyme and potatoes and cook, stirring, for a few minutes. Add the chicken broth and bring to a boil. Lower the heat, add salt to taste, and simmer until the potatoes are almost tender, about 15 minutes. Add the corn and milk and heat until simmering.

■ In a small bowl, stir the butter and flour together to make a smooth paste. Add a cupful of the hot soup to the paste, and whisk until smooth. Stir the mixture into the soup and simmer until thickened. Season with salt and pepper and add the parsley.

ROASTED RED PEPPERS

■

Sweet and smoky fresh roasted red peppers are simple to prepare. First, put some fleshy red bell peppers directly over a burner or grill, turning them until they are evenly blackened and blistered. Put the peppers in a paper bag and fold down the top, or set aside under a bowl until cool (the steam helps loosen the pepper skins). With your fingers, strip away the burned skins. Cut out the stems with a sharp knife and remove the seeds and white membranes. Tear or slice the peppers into strips. Cover with olive oil and store in a container and keep cool.

Lemon Chicken Wings

SERVES 4
PREPARATION: 15 minutes
COOKING: 40 minutes

These golden wings spiked with garlic and a burst of fresh lemon are ideal for picnic lunches or casual hors d'oeuvres.

2 pounds chicken wings, wingtips removed and separated at the joint
4 garlic cloves, finely chopped
2 teaspoons cumin seeds
3 lemons
¼ cup olive oil
Salt
Freshly ground pepper

■ Preheat the oven to 400°F.

■ Put chicken, garlic, and cumin seed in a large noncorrosive dish. Squeeze the juice of two lemons over the wings and add the oil. Sprinkle lightly with salt and a generous amount of pepper. Turn pieces thoroughly in the marinade.

■ Cut the remaining lemon into thin slices and place in a baking dish large enough to hold the wings in one layer. Arrange the wings in the dish and cover.

■ Bake the wings, brushing occasionally with the pan juices, until they are golden, about 40 minutes. Serve at room temperature.

Note: For a stronger flavor, marinate the wings in the refrigerator overnight.

Suggested Wine: A crisp dry white such as California Semillon or Sauvignon Blanc.

Tabooleh

SERVES 4 to 6
PREPARATION: 30 minutes

This cracked wheat salad is earthy and refreshing and hard to beat for its simplicity, since it involves no cooking. It's also a wonderful first course for a grilling menu.

2 cups bulgur (processed cracked wheat)
5 or 6 scallions or 1 medium mild onion,
    finely chopped
1/3 cup freshly squeezed lemon juice
    (about 2 lemons)
1/3 cup olive oil
1 cup chopped fresh parsley
2 to 3 tablespoons chopped fresh mint
    (optional)
Salt
1 or 2 ripe fresh tomatoes, seeded,
    chopped, and drained
1 cucumber, seeded, chopped, and
    drained

■ Put the bulgur in a mixing bowl and cover with hot water. Set aside for 30 minutes, or until the bulgur is swelled and chewy but tender.

■ Drain the bulgur in a fine sieve, squeeze out the excess moisture, and turn out into a mixing bowl. Add the scallions, lemon juice, olive oil, parsley, and mint. Toss well, season to taste with salt, and toss well again. Adjust seasoning if necessary; the salad should be distinctly lemony. Add the tomatoes and cucumber, and toss to combine.

Variation: Soak the bulgur in tomato juice or freshly squeezed orange juice instead of water. Add a handful of currants to the salad.

Walnut Shortbread

MAKES 8 large triangles
PREPARATION: 15 minutes
COOKING: 20 minutes

Delight your crew with this easy recipe for rich, nutty cookies.

1/2 pound (2 sticks) unsalted butter,
    softened
1 cup confectioners' sugar
2 teaspoons vanilla extract or
    2 tablespoons Cointreau
2 cups all-purpose flour
1/4 teaspoon salt
1 cup finely chopped walnuts
1/2 cup coarsely broken walnuts
Sugar (optional)

■ Preheat the oven to 325°F.

■ Beat the butter in a mixing bowl with a wooden spoon until creamy. Beat in the confectioners' sugar and vanilla. Stir in the flour and salt. Add the chopped walnuts and mix with your fingers to form a dough.

■ Pat the dough into a 9-inch round cake pan or shape a 9-inch round on a cookie sheet. Lightly press the remaining walnut pieces into the surface of the dough and score the round into pie-shaped wedges with a sharp knife or the tines of a fork. Prick the dough in several places and make a decorative edge with the fork. Sprinkle the dough with granulated sugar, if desired.

■ Bake the shortbread until it is firm and lightly browned, about 20 minutes. Allow the shortbread to cool slightly, then cut into wedges as scored. Store the cookies in an airtight container.

"I began to brush up on the mysteries of sailing a boat after an unfortunate evening when a lady who sat next to me at dinner turned to me and said, 'Do you reef in your gaff-topsails when you are close-hauled or do you let go the mizzen-top bowlines and crossjack braces?' She took me for a sailor and not a landlubber, and of course I hadn't the slightest idea what she was talking about."

James Thurber

Catching the Blues

O n a warm afternoon in late September, the shimmering Chesapeake seems vast. The shoreline glows with the tawny colors of autumn foliage. With the crowds gone, only a handful of boats remain—the long, low workboats for hauling crabs and the small powerboats with fishing rods quivering in the wind. It's a perfect day to troll for bluefish.

On board the powerboats, marine radios crackle as sportfishermen listen intently for news of where the blues are running. Experienced eyes scan the horizon for working birds that circle and dive for bait fish, a telltale sign that blues are moving beneath. Casting and jigging, trying new lures, people wait patiently for a nibble, enjoying the ritual and each other's company.

Lunch is an important part of these outings, especially if the fish aren't running. Some fishermen on the bay are renowned for the lunches they serve and compete good-naturedly to put on the best spread.

For fishing picnics, the food should be substantial and easy to serve and eat. Chicken salad can be spread on bread for a quick sandwich or leisurely munched throughout the day. You might also tuck a hearty pâté into the cooler for late in the afternoon, when the weather has turned cool and you're heading home with the day's catch.

Chicken Salad with Walnuts

MAKES ABOUT 6 cups
PREPARATION: 15 minutes

Hearty enough to serve alone, this crunchy chicken salad is also terrific on whole grain bread.

4 cups (about 2 pounds) diced cooked chicken
1 cup chopped celery
3 to 4 scallions, finely sliced, or 1/4 cup finely chopped onion
Salt
Freshly ground pepper
3/4 cup mayonnaise
3/4 cup sour cream or plain yogurt
2 tablespoons freshly squeezed lemon juice or herbed vinegar
Pinch nutmeg
1 cup coarsely broken walnuts
1/2 cup chopped mango chutney (optional)
1/4 cup currants or raisins (optional)

■ Combine the chicken, celery, and scallions in a large mixing bowl. Season to taste with salt and pepper.

■ Add the mayonnaise, sour cream, and lemon juice and toss lightly, combining well. Sprinkle the salad with nutmeg, and fold in the nuts, chutney, and currants. Cover and chill the salad until ready to serve.

Suggested Wine: Vouvray or Sauvignon Blanc.

A fisherman's picnic of salads and cheese ready to eat.

ABOVE: Impromptu hors d'oeuvres of brie on pumpernickel with apple slices.

LEFT: Chicken salad with walnuts, Italian eggplant salad, and grated carrot salad.

BALI BENDER

∎

A sure way to kill fish is to pour a big splash of high-proof alcohol such as vodka or gin into its gills. Elizabeth saw this technique used on a wildly thrashing 25-pound mahimahi during a Pacific passage. It never knew what hit him.

FISHY BUSINESS

∎

Filleting fish isn't tricky. Just make sure you have a sharp filleting knife. If you intend to use the fillets only, there is no need to gut the fish.

1. Holding the fish by the tail, scrape the scales with the back of the knife, working against them from tail to head. Rinse the fish quickly.

2. Place the fish on its side with the back toward you and cut along the length of the backbone from head to tail. Holding the knife flat against the bones, cut the fish just under the gills, above the tail, and along the belly, simultaneously peeling back the fillet with the other hand.

3. Turn the fish over and repeat for the second fillet.

4. Place each fillet skin side down on a cutting board. Slide the knife between the skin and the flesh at the tail end, exposing enough flesh to anchor it with your fingertips. Slide the knife at an angle between the skin and flesh, cutting away from you while pulling the skin back with the other hand.

5. Trim the fillets.

Grated Carrot Salad

SERVES 4 to 6
PREPARATION: 15 minutes

A bright salad that stays fresh and crisp all day.

6 large carrots (about 1 pound)
1 tablespoon freshly squeezed lemon juice
4 tablespoons orange juice
6 to 8 tablespoons olive oil or vegetable oil
1 tablespoon grated orange rind (optional)
½ teaspoon sugar
Salt
Cayenne (ground red) pepper

∎ Peel the carrots and grate them coarsely into a large mixing bowl. Add the lemon juice, orange juice, oil, orange rind, and sugar. Add the salt and a light dusting of cayenne pepper. Toss lightly and store in a cool place until ready to serve.

Variation: The sweet, clean taste of carrots blends well with many contrasting ingredients. Try adding a teaspoonful of cumin seed; a handful of currants and some finely sliced red onion; chopped nuts such as pecans, pine nuts, or hazelnuts; thinly sliced scallions, walnuts, and crumbled blue cheese.

Italian Eggplant Salad

SERVES 4 to 6
PREPARATION: 15 minutes
COOKING: 45 minutes

This glossy, colorful, and richly flavored salad is one of our favorites.

2 pounds small tender eggplant
½ cup (approximately) olive oil or vegetable oil
Salt
¼ cup red wine vinegar
1 teaspoon sugar
2 garlic cloves, finely chopped
½ cup sliced roasted red peppers (page 84)
½ teaspoon dried marjoram or oregano
¼ cup currants
2 tablespoons capers
3 to 4 tablespoons finely chopped celery leaves

Garnish
Whole celery leaves

∎ Preheat the oven to 400°F.

∎ Cut each eggplant lengthwise into quarters. Cut the quarters into 2-inch sections. Place the eggplant in a shallow baking pan large enough to hold the pieces in one layer. Add the olive oil and toss to coat the pieces generously.

∎ Bake the eggplant, turning the pieces every 15 minutes, about 40 minutes, until tender and golden brown.

∎ Remove the eggplant from the oven, pour off any excess oil, and allow to cool in the pan. Sprinkle the eggplant lightly with salt, vinegar, and sugar and turn gently. Fold in the remaining ingredients. Scattter a few celery leaves on top of the salad as decoration. Serve at room temperature.

Variation: Grilling instead of baking the eggplant will give the salad an irresistible smoky flavor.

Dorothy's Chicken Liver Pâté

MAKES ABOUT 3 cups
PREPARATION: 30 minutes
COOKING: 15 minutes

Elizabeth's friend Dorothy, with whom she sailed on a nerve-racking stormy passage across the Gulf Stream to Abaco, knows a thing or two about good food. This smooth, rich, redolent pâté is from her capacious recipe file.

½ pound bacon, cut into ½-inch pieces
1 apple, peeled, cored, and coarsely chopped
1 small onion, peeled and finely chopped
1 pound chicken livers, trimmed and patted dry
½ cup robust dry red wine
1 teaspoon dried tarragon
Salt
Freshly ground pepper
1 to 2 tablespoons chopped fresh parsley
2 tablespoons unsalted butter, melted

■ Sauté the bacon in a large skillet over medium heat until the fat runs. Add the apple and onion and sauté until softened. Add the livers and toss until they begin to turn gray. Add the wine and tarragon. Raise the heat to high and allow the wine to bubble until it is reduced by half. Remove the pan from the heat and season to taste with salt and pepper.

■ Add the parsley and mash the mixture into a coarse paste with a fork. If desired, purée the mixture further with a food mill or food processor.

■ Spoon the pâté into crocks. Seal with melted butter and chill several hours. Store for at least one day to allow the flavors to blend. Serve with hot sliced French bread or crisp crackers. The pâté will keep for 1 week in the refrigerator.

Old-Fashioned Pickled Fish

(ALTERNATE RECIPE)

FOR 2 pounds of fish fillets
PREPARATION: 15 minutes plus 24 hours marination
COOKING: 10 minutes

Pickling is an easy, delicious way to preserve extra fish. Serve pickled fish with an herbed rice salad and sliced tomatoes for lunch.

2 medium onions, sliced
2 medium carrots, sliced
2 bay leaves
4 whole allspice
2 teaspoons whole black peppercorns
2 garlic cloves, lightly crushed
2 teaspoons salt
2 cups water
1 cup cider or white wine vinegar
½ cup vegetable oil
2 pounds boneless, skinless fish fillets, such as bluefish (see Note)

■ Combine all the ingredients except the fish in a saucepan. Bring the liquid to a boil and simmer for 5 minutes. Allow the mixture to cool.

■ Sterilize wide-mouthed glass canning jars and their lids in a pot of boiling water for several minutes. Fill the jars loosely with fish and cover with the marinade.

■ Seal the jars and let stand for 24 hours in a cool place. The fish will keep, refrigerated, for up to 2 weeks.

Note: You may choose to brown the fish in oil before covering with the marinade.

BLUEFISH FEAST

■

We're fond of serving the day's catch many ways, including:

· *Sautéed with Lemon and Capers:* Season bluefish fillets with salt and pepper, dust them with flour, and sauté in butter until done. Remove the fish and keep warm. Meanwhile, cut the peel and pith from 1 or 2 lemons; thinly slice the lemons crosswise, discarding any seeds; and add the slices to the pan with additional butter and a tablespoon each of capers and chopped parsley. When sizzling, pour the sauce over the fish.

· *Grilled with Tomatoes and Onions:* Place bluefish fillets skin side down on a sheet of lightly oiled aluminum foil. Sprinkle the fish with salt and pepper; cover the fillets with overlapping rounds of thinly sliced tomato, cucumber, and onion; sprinkle the vegetables with salt and pepper and lemon juice or white wine; dot with butter; and broil or cook on a covered grill until done.

· *Grilled with Aquavit:* Diagonally score each side of a whole bluefish, making 4 or 5 parallel slashes about ¼ inch deep. Crush 1 tablespoon dill or fennel seed with 2 teaspoons salt and mix with ½ cup chopped fresh dill. Rub the mixture onto the fish and into the slashes. Sprinkle the fish with 4 to 5 tablespoons Aquavit. Marinate the fish 30 minutes. Grill, preferably in a wire grilling basket, until the fish tests done.

ENTERTAINING ABOARD

Hors d'Oeuvres in the Harbor

M E N U

Tomato Croustades

Sardines on Black Bread with Mustard Butter

Steamed Sausage and Potatoes

Herbed Marinated Cheese

∎

"I had to sink my yacht to make the guests go home."
F. Scott Fitzgerald

Although we'd hardly invite a carload of strangers in a parking lot home to dinner, when we are cruising, the experience of being in a lovely location is enough to dispel our landlocked sensibilities. After setting anchor, we often row over to an interesting-looking crew moored nearby and invite them aboard for cocktails. From Block Island to Bermuda, we've met the liveliest, most adventurous people this way.

We know a film producer's wife in Newport Beach, California, who doesn't even bother to travel to entertain topside. With the boat moored a stone's throw from the house, she and her husband invite business clients aboard for hors d'oeuvres at sunset. "It relaxes them so much," she says, "that they don't even realize we haven't left the harbor."

Whatever the circumstances, asking people on board for cocktails on a warm, clear evening is a special invitation. But what should you serve? Fine cheeses and crackers are always welcome, but there are many other uncomplicated possibilities. Even plain ingredients such as garlic sausages and steamed potatoes can be transformed by artful cutting and serving with a piquant sauce.

Of necessity, the food should be easy to prepare; a galley is not an ideal place to fuss with tiny cherry tomatoes filled with smoked salmon mousse. Use the freshest ingredients available, taking time to prepare them attractively. Sprinkle a line of paprika, for example, across a pale crab dip to give it drama. Decorate a platter with a cluster of fresh fruit or flowers. Make a geometric design on a dark eggplant dip with crisp celery leaves. Or, serve a spicy dip in a hollowed-out cabbage or pepper.

We usually select hors d'oeuvres that can be prepared ahead of time to allow more time with guests. Raw vegetables, for example, will stay fresh for several hours when covered with a damp towel. If we want to serve hot hors d'oeuvres, we limit ourselves to one or two that can be managed conveniently.

Serving equipment always poses a problem on boats, where space is at a premium. A few all-purpose platters come in handy, as do cutting boards, bread boards, salad bowls, and flat baskets. When chartering, we camouflage unattractive equipment with big cabbage or lettuce leaves, palm fronds, or unusual shells.

Tomato Croustades

MAKES 24 pieces
PREPARATION: 20 minutes
COOKING: 10 minutes

Crunchy fried bread scented with garlic is delicious, especially when topped with a chopped tomato salad.

2 or 3 ripe tomatoes, seeded and finely
chopped
1 to 2 tablespoons chopped fresh parsley
1 to 2 tablespoons finely chopped onion or
scallions
Black olives, pitted and slivered (optional)
Red wine vinegar
Salt
Freshly ground pepper
1 long thin loaf French bread
Olive oil
2 garlic cloves, peeled and lightly crushed

■ Combine the tomatoes, parsley, onion, and olives in a small bowl. Sprinkle on a few drops of vinegar and season with salt and pepper. Allow to marinate for 30 minutes at room temperature.

■ Cut the bread crosswise into ¼-inch slices. Pour oil into a large skillet to a depth of ⅛ inch and heat over medium-low heat. Add the garlic and sizzle gently for a few minutes. Brush the bread slices generously with the oil. Place a layer of bread slices in the pan and fry gently until golden brown. Turn and brown the other side. Transfer the slices to paper towels or a folded brown paper bag to drain. Fry remaining slices.

■ Mound the tomato mixture onto the croustades and set on a platter until ready to serve. The juices from the tomatoes will soak into the bread, softening it slightly.

Sardines on Black Bread with Mustard Butter

MAKES 12 small sandwiches
PREPARATION: 20 minutes

These open-faced sandwiches are best made with firm, European-style dark bread. Or sandwich the sardines and cucumber slices between slices of the buttered bread and cut into triangles or squares.

1 tablespoon Dijon mustard
1 teaspoon dried dill
Few drops lemon juice
4 tablespoons unsalted butter, softened

Freshly ground pepper
Thinly sliced cucumber
White wine or herbed vinegar
Thinly sliced black bread or rye bread
2 4½-ounce cans brisling sardines or
other small sardines

■ Combine the mustard and dill in a small bowl. Add the lemon juice and the butter. Set aside for 10 minutes. Mix the ingredients with a fork until smooth, and season with pepper.

■ Combine the cucumbers and vinegar in a bowl and season with pepper.

■ Spread the mustard butter on each slice of bread. Cut away the crusts, making neat squares, and cut again into rectangles long enough to hold the sardines. Place a few cucumber slices on the bread and place a whole sardine on top.

Steamed Sausage and Potatoes

SERVES 6
PREPARATION: 10 minutes
COOKING: 20 minutes

Steamed potatoes may seem uninspiring, but when freshly cooked and still warm, they are surprisingly good, especially with little bowls of condiments such as horseradish mayonnaise, green sauce, or a zesty vinaigrette.

1 pound kielbasa or similar spicy sausage
6 new potatoes, cut into wedges

Garnish
Olives
Gherkin pickles

■ Place the sausage and potatoes in a steamer set over a large pot of boiling water. Cover the pot and steam until the potatoes are just tender, about 10 minutes.

■ When the sausage is cool enough to handle, slice it thinly and pile onto a platter with a mound of potatoes. Garnish with the olives and pickles. Serve warm or at room temperature.

QUICK DIPS
■

Cream cheese is an excellent base for strongly flavored ingredients. Make a creamy dip or spread by combining softened cream cheese with sour cream or mayonnaise and one of the following:

· smoked salmon

· smoked oysters or clams

· crabmeat, curry, and scallions

· Cheddar, bacon, and beer

· dried beef

· liverwurst

· blue cheese

· chutney and curry

· spicy salsa

■ Place the cheese on a serving dish and drizzle with olive oil. Serve with crisp crackers or toasted French bread rounds.

Note: An excellent way to preserve this cheese is to immerse it in olive oil in an airtight container. After eating the cheese, strain the oil and use it for salad dressings, garlic bread, or croutons.

Variation: Other flavorful coatings for goat cheese include crisp bread crumbs, crushed black peppercorns, or *herbes de Provence.*

Potted Sardines
(ALTERNATE RECIPE)

MAKES 1½ cups
PREPARATION: 15 minutes

Serve this tasty concoction with crisp crackers.

2 4½-ounce cans smoked sardines packed in oil, drained
8 tablespoons (1 stick) unsalted butter, softened
2 tablespoons lemon juice (about ½ lemon)
Tabasco or cayenne (ground red) pepper
Freshly ground pepper
1 to 2 teaspoons brandy or bourbon (optional)
Melted butter

Garnish
Fresh herb sprigs, capers, or red onion slice

■ Combine the sardines, butter, and lemon juice in a bowl. Season with Tabasco, pepper, and brandy. Mash into a coarse paste with a fork, adjust seasoning.

■ Spoon the mixture into a pretty dish or crock and smooth the top. Cover with a little melted butter and decorate the top with herb sprigs, a few capers, or a slice of red onion pulled into a fan.

Variation: Add a little mustard, a tablespoon of finely chopped onion, or a clove of chopped garlic to the sardines along with the seasoning.

At dockside cocktail parties, we like to pull out the stops with crystal glasses and candlelight.

OPPOSITE TOP: Colorful tomato croustades are light and summery. OPPOSITE BOTTOM: Serve these Scandinavian-style canapes with lemon wedges.

Herbed Marinated Cheese

MAKES one 10-ounce cheese
PREPARATION: 10 minutes

1 teaspoon crushed dried rosemary
1 teaspoon crushed dried thyme
1 teaspoon crushed dried marjoram
¼ cup chopped fresh parsley
¼ teaspoon crushed red pepper
¼ teaspoon coarsely ground pepper
1 10-ounce log fresh white goat cheese such as Montrachet
Olive oil

■ Mix the herbs, pepper flakes, and pepper on a plate or a shallow bowl. Roll the cheese in the mixture until well coated and pat the herbs into the surface of the cheese.

Dock Party

All along the Thousand Islands of the Saint Lawrence River, powerboats are a way of life. Restaurants have boat slips along with parking lots, and the mailman delivers by boat. The same families have been summering here for generations, and children grow up with boats—driving them, playing with them, waterskiing from them. Cocktail parties at the dock are popular, and an ideal way to entertain friends on a beautiful summer evening at The River.

Spicy Skewered Beef with Peanut Sauce

MAKES ABOUT 15 skewers
PREPARATION: 20 minutes and 30
  minutes marinating
COOKING: 10 minutes

Serve these spicy bite-size kebabs at room temperature or hot off the grill.

> *1½ pounds lean tender beef, such as*
>   *sirloin or top round*
> *2 garlic cloves, finely chopped*
> *3 tablespoons soy sauce*
> *3 tablespoons vegetable oil*
> *½ cup cream of coconut*
> *1 teaspoon ground cumin*
> *1 teaspoon freshly ground pepper*
> *½ teaspoon crushed red pepper*
> *1 teaspoon grated lemon rind*
> *Peanut Sauce (recipe follows)*
> *Vegetable oil*

■ Soak bamboo skewers in water for at least 1 hour.

■ Prepare the grill (page 13).

■ Cut the beef into 1-inch cubes and combine with the remaining ingredients in a large mixing bowl. Mix well and set aside for at least 30 minutes to marinate.

■ Spear 2 or 3 beef cubes on each skewer. Broil 8 to 10 minutes, turning occasionally, until the meat is well browned. Pile the skewers on a platter or in a basket lined with large lettuce leaves or cabbage leaves, if desired. Serve with Peanut Sauce for dipping.

Note: This marinade is also delicious with chicken, lamb, or pork.

Peanut Sauce

MAKES ABOUT 1½ cups
PREPARATION: 5 minutes
COOKING: 5 minutes

> *½ cup smooth peanut butter*
> *1 cup water*
> *1 garlic clove, finely chopped*
> *2 teaspoons brown sugar*
> *2 tablespoons soy sauce*
> *1 tablespoon freshly squeezed lemon juice*
> *¼ teaspoon crushed red pepper*

■ Put the peanut butter in a small saucepan. Add the water by the spoonful, stirring after each addition until smooth.

■ Heat the mixture over low heat until it is slightly thickened. Add the remaining ingredients, stir well, and remove from the heat.

Grilled Skewered Chicken with Green Sauce

(ALTERNATE RECIPE)

MAKES ABOUT 12 skewers
PREPARATION: 10 minutes
COOKING: 10 minutes

The sharp herbal flavor of this vividly green parsley sauce complements grilled or poached meats, sausages, fish, and chicken. Make the sauce at home and bring it aboard as a versatile condiment.

1 pound boneless, skinless chicken breasts
Salt
Freshly ground pepper
1 teaspoon dried marjoram
1 garlic clove, finely chopped
5 tablespoons lemon juice (about 2
*   lemons)*
¼ cup olive oil
Green Sauce (recipe follows)

■ Soak bamboo skewers in water for at least 1 hour to prevent burning.

■ Prepare the grill (page 13).

■ Cut the chicken into 1-inch chunks, season to taste with salt and pepper, and toss with the remaining ingredients. Marinate for at least 30 minutes.

■ Spear 2 or 3 pieces of chicken on each skewer. Broil or grill the chicken, turning frequently and brushing occasionally with the marinade, about 8 minutes, or until golden brown. Serve warm or at room temperature with a dish of Green Sauce for dipping.

Green Sauce

MAKES ABOUT 1½ cups

2 garlic cloves
2 tablespoons Dijon mustard
2 tablespoons capers, drained
1 to 2 teaspoons anchovy paste
1 bunch fresh parsley leaves (about 2
*   cups, loosely packed)*
2 to 3 tablespoons white wine vinegar
½ cup olive oil

■ Combine the garlic, mustard, capers, and anchovy paste in a food processor or blender until finely chopped. Add the parsley and process until finely chopped. Add the vinegar and, with the motor running, slowly pour in the oil, taking care not to overblend the sauce.

■ Cover the sauce with a thin film of oil and store in a container. The sauce will keep up to 2 weeks if well-covered and chilled.

Duble's Deviled Eggs

MAKES 12 halves
PREPARATION: 15 minutes
COOKING: 10 minutes

A hit on family cruises, this recipe comes from Jennifer's brother-in-law, Chris Duble.

6 eggs
3 tablespoons mayonnaise
2 teaspoons Dijon mustard
1 teaspoon curry powder
1 teaspoon dried dill, or 1 tablespoon
*   chopped fresh dill, parsley, or chives*
Paprika

■ Place the eggs in a medium saucepan and add cold water to cover. Bring the water to a boil over high heat. Lower the heat and simmer for about 10 minutes. Drain the eggs and cover with cold water. Peel the eggs when they are cool.

■ Cut each egg in half lengthwise. Carefully remove the yolks and place them in a small mixing bowl. Set aside the whites. Crush the yolks with a fork and add the mayonnaise, mustard, curry powder, and dill. Mix well and mound the mixture lightly into the egg whites. Sprinkle each egg with paprika, and keep cool until ready to serve.

Variation: Substitute 1 or 2 tablespoons Green Sauce (page 97) for the dill and curry. Or add mashed sardines or tuna to the egg yolk mixture.

ENTERTAINING ABOARD

OPPOSITE: Guests arrive by classic wooden power-boats for a dockside cocktail party in the Thousand Islands.

Lemony chick-pea dip with toasted pita triangles can easily serve a crowd.

Succulent shrimp ready to be pickled.

Grilled skewered chicken.

Poisson Crû

SERVES 6 to 8
PREPARATION: 15 minutes

A delightful Tahitian recipe for marinated raw fish.

> *1 pound raw firm fish, such as tuna or*
> *grouper*
> *½ cup freshly squeezed lime juice (about*
> *6 limes)*
> *Salt*
> *1 cup coconut milk*
> *1 teaspoon dried oregano*
> *1 or 2 thinly sliced chiles or ½ teaspoon*
> *crushed red pepper*
> *1 small onion, thinly sliced*

■ Cut the fish into bite-size pieces and place them in a noncorrosive dish with the lime juice. Sprinkle the fish lightly with salt and marinate for at least 1 hour, turning the pieces occasionally. The fish will whiten as the acid from the lime juice "cooks" the flesh. Stir in the coconut milk, oregano, chiles, and onion, and marinate for 1 hour more.

Note: Turn this dish into a summer lunch with sliced tomatoes and cucumbers.

Gravlax with Mustard Sauce

MAKES ABOUT 2½ pounds
PREPARATION: 10 minutes plus 3 days curing

This Scandinavian method of curing salmon and trout can also be used for bluefish with excellent results.

> *1 6-pound bluefish, filleted*
> *3 tablespoons salt*
> *¼ cup sugar*
> *1 tablespoon crushed black peppercorns*
> *1 tablespoon crushed fennel seeds*
> *2 bunches fresh dill, separated into sprigs*
> *(large stems removed)*
> *Mustard Sauce (recipe follows)*

■ Rub the cut side of each fillet with salt, sugar, peppercorns, and fennel seed. Place one fillet skin side down in a nonreactive container large enough to hold the fish comfortably (a Pyrex baking dish works well). Pack the dill sprigs onto one of the fillets. Arrange the other fillet on top, skin side up. Cover the fish with plastic wrap and weight with a cutting board held down by cans of food or other items weighing several pounds.

■ Refrigerate 3 days, carefully turning the fish daily. (The fish will take on a translucent look and liquid will accumulate in the dish.)

■ To serve, scrape away the herbs and spices and slice the fish into wide, paper-thin slices as you would smoked salmon. Serve with black bread, butter, and Mustard Sauce. The fish will keep, refrigerated, up to 1 week.

Mustard Sauce

MAKES ¾ cup
PREPARATION: 5 minutes

> *¼ cup Dijon mustard*
> *1 tablespoon brown sugar*
> *2 tablespoons white wine vinegar*
> *2 teaspoons crushed brine-cured green*
> *peppercorns*
> *¼ cup vegetable oil*
> *1 to 2 tablespoons heavy cream*
> *¼ cup chopped fresh dill, or 2 tablespoons*
> *dry tarragon, chervil, or chives*

■ Combine all ingredients and stir until blended. Store in the refrigerator.

Note: This sauce is also delicious with smoked meat and fish.

COCONUT MILK

■

Pacific islanders produce coconut milk on a small scale, packaging it in small glass bottles. If you're not cruising the Pacific, you can make coconut milk easily with a blender or food processor.

Heat a large coconut for about 10 minutes in a 300°F. oven to loosen the meat from the shell. Crack the shell, pry out the meat, and pare away the brown skin. Break the meat into small chunks and grind them in a blender with enough hot water to keep the mixture moving until the meat is finely chopped. Pour the mixture into a fine strainer and squeeze the liquid from the pulp.

If you don't have a blender, coarsely grate the coconut, then soak it in hot water. Or use packaged shredded unsweetened coconut.

However you obtain it, coconut milk should be refrigerated if not used within a day.

Pickled Shrimp

(ALTERNATE RECIPE)

MAKES 2 quarts
PREPARATION: 20 minutes
COOKING: 10 minutes

*2 to 3 pounds freshly boiled shrimp (recipe
    follows)*
2 medium red onions, peeled and sliced
*2 lemons, sliced crosswise into 1/8-inch-
    thick slices*
4 bay leaves
2 sticks cinnamon
6 whole cloves
2 teaspoons whole black peppercorns
2 garlic cloves, crushed
2 cups oil
1 1/2 cups white vinegar
1/2 cup dry or medium sherry
1/2 cup water
1/2 cup brown sugar

■ Peel and devein the shrimp if desired. Layer the shrimp, onion, and lemon slices in 2 quart-size Mason jars, adding the bay leaves, cinnamon sticks, cloves, peppercorns, and garlic intermittently.

■ Combine the remaining ingredients. Heat in a saucepan over medium-high heat, stirring until the liquid comes to a boil. Pour over the shrimp. Seal the jars tightly and refrigerate the shrimp for at least 24 hours before serving.

Boiled Shrimp

■ To cook several pounds fresh shrimp, fill a large pot with fresh water twice the volume of the unshelled shrimp. Add to the water a small handful of salt, a sliced lemon or two, several bay leaves, cloves, chiles, fresh parsley, onions, and garlic cloves. Bring the water to a rolling boil and boil for 5 minutes.

■ Meanwhile, rinse and drain the shrimp. Add the shrimp to the boiling water, stir well, and cook 2 to 3 minutes (less if the shrimp are tiny). Remove one shrimp and test for doneness by biting into it. The shrimp should be just barely done when you drain them, because they will continue to cook off the heat.

■ Drain the shrimp, immerse them immediately in a bucket of sea water, and drain again.

Parslied Chick-Pea Dip

(ALTERNATE RECIPE)

MAKES ABOUT 3 cups
PREPARATION: 15 minutes

We like to serve this lemony green dip with toasted triangles of pita bread.

*1 16-ounce can chick-peas, drained and
    rinsed*
1/2 cup tahini (sesame paste)
*1/3 to 1/2 cup lemon juice (about 2 to 3
    lemons)*
1/2 cup or more olive oil
3 to 4 garlic cloves, minced
*1/2 cup finely chopped fresh parsely, plus
    additional for garnish*
Salt
Paprika

■ Purée the chick-peas in a food mill, food processor, or blender. (If using a food processor or blender, purée the chick-peas with the tahini and some of the lemon juice.)

■ Combine the puréed chick-peas and tahini in a mixing bowl. Stir in lemon juice to taste and 1/2 cup olive oil. Add the garlic and parsley and stir until the mixture is smooth and flecked with green. Taste for seasoning and add salt and lemon juice if desired. Decorate the surface of the dip with pinches of parsley and sprinkle it with paprika. Drizzle a thread of olive oil over the surface in a zigzag pattern. Serve at room temperature.

SEA COOKING

■

Seagoing Polynesians have cooked with seawater for centuries. If you're cruising in remote areas where the water is clean, conserve your fresh water supply by boiling eggs and unpeeled vegetables (such as carrots, potatoes or corn) in seawater. When cooking rice, oatmeal, or pasta, try adding 1 part seawater to 3 parts fresh water.

Caribbean Christmas

M E N U

*Caribbean Lobsters
with Limes*

*Lizard's Cucumber
Salad*

*Sautéed Bananas with
Rum*

Gingerbread Men

■

OPPOSITE: Our Christmas
dinner in Mustique fea-
tured Caribbean lobsters
with key limes, not to mention stockings and tree
trimmings brought from
home.

As New En-
glanders, we
are used to
traditional Christmas holidays filled with
caroling parties, crunchy snow, blazing
fires, and candlelight dinners. But while
spending a Christmas in the Grenadine
Islands, we loved the liberating effects of
a tropical holiday, in which cherished old
traditions could be replaced by marvelous
new ones, such as swimming and snor-
keling in turquoise waters before Christmas dinner.

Decorating the boat will get you into
the holiday spirit. If you're feeling ambi-
tious, you might even hang a stocking or
two. For our holiday, we tucked some
glittery ornaments into our duffel bags
(this is not the place for heirlooms!), as
well as a few small gifts and the gingerbread men that we had baked at home.

Many good restaurants are open to
yachtsmen on Christmas day, but we preferred the intimacy of dining on board in
a palm-fringed lagoon. Preparing a simple yet sumptuous feast wasn't much
work and provided a great excuse to visit
the colorful open markets found in the
islands. After an early lobster dinner, we
enjoyed a lazy afternoon of swimming
and sunbathing. Then, as the sun disappeared into the sea, we lit candles and
gathered in the cockpit to exchange gifts
over coffee and cordials, nibbling on our
gingerbread men.

Caribbean Lobsters with Limes

SERVES 4
PREPARATION: 10 minutes
COOKING: 15 minutes

The rich, white meat of the spiny lobster is a special treat. Its mild, sweet flavor is enhanced by a squirt of lime and light mayonnaise. If you're lucky enough to have leftovers, use the cooked meat in a salad or for Lobster Creole (page 105).

*4 spiny lobsters of equal size,
    approximately 1½ to 2 pounds each
Mayonnaise (recipe follows)*

Garnish
Limes

■ Fill a large pot with fresh or sea water and bring it to a rolling boil over high heat (see Note). Plunge the lobsters into the pot head first, taking care not to crowd them, so they will cook evenly. Cover the pot and cook 15 minutes, or until lobsters turn scarlet. Remove the lobsters from the pot and drain.

■ Using a folded towel to protect your hands while handling the lobsters, with a large, heavy knife split the lobsters in half lengthwise. Remove and discard the sandy sac from the head of each lobster. Serve the lobsters hot or cold. Garnish with lime and serve with mayonnaise.

Note: If your boat is not equipped with a pot large enough to boil four lobsters at once, cook them individually and serve them cold. (This also gives you the flexibility of a few hours in which to prepare dinner.) Or, undercook the lobsters slightly, allow them to cool, then split them and finish on the grill, basting well with melted butter, lime, and perhaps a few tablespoons of such chopped fresh herbs as thyme, parsley, and chives.

Suggested Wine: A rich, fragrant white such as Puligny or Montrachet.

Mayonnaise

MAKES ABOUT 2 cups
PREPARATION: 15 minutes

Making mayonnaise is simple; just be sure the ingredients are at room temperature and add the oil to the egg yolks slowly at the beginning, incorporating each drop before adding more. The entire process should take about 15 minutes. The boiling water beaten in at the end stabilizes the mayonnaise. The mayonnaise will be thin at first, but it will thicken after standing for an hour or so. If you are making an herb mayonnaise with dried herbs, steep them first in lemon juice to revive them.

*3 egg yolks
2 teaspoons cider or white wine vinegar
½ teaspoon salt
2 or 3 drops Tabasco
1 teaspoon Dijon mustard (optional)
1½ to 1¾ cups olive oil or vegetable oil,
    or a combination
1 to 2 tablespoons freshly squeezed lemon
    juice or lime juice
1 to 2 tablespoons boiling water*

■ Beat the egg yolks, vinegar, salt, Tabasco, and mustard in a large mixing bowl with a wire whisk. Add about half the oil drop by drop, beating constantly until the mixture is very thick and smooth. Beat in 1 tablespoon lemon juice, then add the remaining oil in a thin stream, beating constantly. Taste and adjust seasoning with more salt and lemon juice.

■ Add a tablespoon or two of boiling water to the mayonnaise and beat until the mixture is smooth.

Lobster Creole

(ALTERNATE RECIPE)

SERVES 4 to 6
PREPARATION: 20 minutes
COOKING: 40 minutes

The classic version of this recipe involves more steps than most people would ever consider on land, much less in a galley. Happily, this departure from tradition is delicious and well suited for small work spaces. Shrimp, chicken, and fish are also terrific simmered in this sauce.

½ to 1 cup chopped cooked ham
¼ cup olive oil
2 garlic cloves, finely chopped
2 green bell peppers, stemmed, seeded, and finely chopped
1 to 2 small chiles, seeded and finely chopped, or ½ to 1 teaspoon crushed red pepper, or Tabasco to taste
1 celery stalk with leaves, chopped
2 medium onions, peeled and finely chopped
½ teaspoon dried oregano
1 bay leaf
1 cup dry white wine
2 cups finely chopped and seeded canned tomatoes
3 to 4 cups 1-inch chunks cooked lobster meat

■ Place the ham and olive oil in a large, heavy pan over medium-high heat. Cook, stirring, until the ham begins to brown. Add the garlic, peppers, chiles, celery, onions, oregano, and bay leaf. Reduce heat to medium and cook, stirring, until the vegetables are softened, about 5 minutes.

■ Add the wine and cook 5 minutes. Add the tomatoes and lower the heat. Simmer the mixture until the sauce has thickened, about 20 minutes.

■ Stir the lobster meat into the sauce and simmer for about 10 minutes. Serve with rice, pasta, or hot, crusty bread.

Lizard's Cucumber Salad

SERVES 4
PREPARATION: 20 minutes

This cool, silken salad is a knockout on a fiercely hot day.

1 garlic clove, crushed
2 to 3 thin slices fresh ginger root
2 tablespoons freshly squeezed lime juice, or white wine vinegar
1 tablespoon sugar
4 to 6 medium cucumbers
Salt
Soy sauce

■ Mix the garlic, ginger, lime juice, and sugar and set the marinade aside. Peel the cucumbers and cut them in half lengthwise. Using a teaspoon, scrape out the seeds. Cut cucumber halves into ⅛-inch-thick slices, place them in a colander, and salt lightly. Allow the cucumbers to drain for 10 minutes, shaking the colander to remove any excess moisture.

■ Combine the cucumbers in a bowl with the marinade and let stand for 20 minutes. Drain the excess liquid from the cucumbers, and discard the garlic and ginger. Serve the cucumbers sprinkled with a few drops soy sauce, if desired.

ON THE ROCKS

■

Basil's Bar on tiny Mustique is a rollicking place where English royalty mingles with rock stars, captains of industry, and the yachting crowd. The specialty drinks are potent, especially after a day in the blazing sun. The affable owner, Basil Charles, shared some of his recipes. Even if you don't visit the island, these drinks will make you feel as though you're there.

· *Mustique Grin:* For 1 drink, blend 1½ ounces green Crème de Menthe, ½ ounce rum, ½ ounce cream of coconut or piña colada mix, and 1 banana with crushed ice. Serve in a tall glass.

· *Mustique Whammy:* For 1 drink, top a tall, ice-filled glass containing 1½ ounces white rum and ½ ounce Triple Sec with orange juice, a dash of grenadine, and a lime and orange wedge. Serve with a cherry.

· *Jump Up and Kiss Me:* For 1 drink, top 1 ounce vodka with fresh coconut water, and add a dash of grenadine .

· *Basil's Highball:* For 1 drink, shake together ⅓ ounce gin, ⅓ ounce Cointreau, ⅓ ounce rum, about ½ ounce lime juice, and 2 teaspoons sugar. Serve over cracked ice in a highball glass.

Beachcombing on the windward shore.

ABOVE: A cool cucumber salad accompanies the rich sweet Caribbean lobster.

RIGHT: Sweet gingerbread men and gaily wrapped presents add a traditional touch to this tropical Christmas dinner.

Sautéed Bananas with Rum

SERVES 6
PREPARATION: 5 minutes
COOKING: 10 minutes

Effortless and elegant, this recipe with its buttery rum sauce elevates bananas to a new plane.

6 firm ripe bananas
4 tablespoons (1/2 stick) unsalted butter
1/3 cup brown sugar
1 to 2 tablespoons freshly squeezed lime juice
Freshly grated nutmeg
1/2 cup light rum, such as Mount Gay or Bacardi Gold

■ Peel the bananas and cut them in half crosswise.

■ Melt the butter over medium-high heat in a skillet large enough to hold the bananas in one layer.

■ Add the bananas and cook, shaking the pan gently, until they are lightly browned all over. Add the sugar and lime juice and sprinkle the bananas with nutmeg. Continue to shake the pan gently for a few minutes until the sugar dissolves. Add the rum. When it is warm, ignite the rum with a match and agitate the pan until the flames die. Serve the bananas immediately, with the pan juices spooned over the top.

Gingerbread Men

MAKES ABOUT 30 cookies
PREPARATION: 45 minutes
COOKING: 10 minutes

12 tablespoons (1 1/2 sticks) unsalted butter, softened
2/3 cup dark brown sugar
1/2 cup molasses
1 egg
1 teaspoon vanilla extract
3 cups all-purpose flour
1/4 teaspoon salt
1 teaspoon cinnamon
2 teaspoons ground ginger
1/2 teaspoon ground cloves
1/2 teaspoon freshly grated nutmeg

Decoration
Red Hot (cinnamon) candies
Currants

■ Beat the butter, adding the sugar gradually, until the mixture is creamy. Add the molasses, egg, and vanilla, and beat until smooth.

■ Combine the dry ingredients and stir well with a whisk. Add the dry ingredients to the butter mixture and blend thoroughly. Chill the dough for about 1 hour.

■ Preheat the oven to 350°F.

■ Roll out the dough to a thickness of about 1/4 inch and cut out shapes with a gingerbread man cookie cutter. Place the cookies on a greased baking sheet about 1 inch apart. Decorate each cookie with Red Hot candies (buttons) and currants (eyes). Make hair for the gingerbread men by forcing small amounts of the dough through a garlic press and gently affixing the strands to the cookies with the edge of a knife.

■ Bake the cookies for about 10 minutes, or until they are lightly browned and firm to the touch. Cool on wire racks before storing. These cookies will keep well in a tightly sealed container.

Tugboat Birthday

Birthdays that are celebrated with fanfare and creativity stand out in our memories: a 21st birthday honored at New York's famed "21" club; a one hundredth birthday barbecue on the beach with hundreds of friends accumulated over a lifetime; a twelfth birthday spent sailing to a budding sailor's favorite island. Intimate or grand, surprise or planned, birthday parties are a great way to pamper and indulge the people you love.

If you will be cruising on someone's birthday, make it a festive day to remember. Before departing, buy colorful streamers and helium balloons to decorate the boat. If the guest of honor is pint-size, pack party hats, noisemakers, Hawaiian leis, etc. It's not much effort and gets everyone into high spirits.

As an added treat, serve the birthday person's favorite food. One three-year-old friend of ours loves shiitake mushrooms and sushi. Yet, when asked to name her favorite food, she exclaimed, "Hotdogs!" Indeed, many of our older friends request familiar childhood dishes —meatloaf and homemade mashed potatoes, butterflied lamb and asparagus— for their day in the sun.

For a birthday party aboard *Puffin II,* a 26-foot Harbor Tug, we cruised to a pretty, isolated spot near Watch Hill, Rhode Island. Most of the group went ashore for a birthday picnic that included our much-requested Nautical Nuggets and Lizard's Cucumber Salad, while a few adults stayed behind to decorate. Returning to the boat an hour later, the children giggled with delight when they saw the dessert: a tugboat cake decorated with Lifesaver portholes and licorice lifelines.

Pink Punch

MAKES ABOUT 2½ quarts
PREPARATION: 10 minutes

1 quart cranberry juice cocktail
2 cups pineapple juice
½ cup orange juice
¼ cup freshly squeezed lemon juice
1 quart ginger ale, chilled

Garnish
Orange and lemon slices (optional)

■ Combine the fruit juices in a large container and chill.

■ Just before serving, stir in the ginger ale. Serve the punch over ice, garnished with orange and lemon slices or other fruit if desired.

M E N U

Pink Punch

Nautical Nuggets

Creamy Potato Salad

Raw Vegetables

Lizard's Cucumber Salad (page 105)

Vanilla Tugboat Cake

■

A bright red tugboat was the perfect stage for a young girl's birthday.

Picnic lunch on the beach included nautical nuggets and lizard's cucumber salad with a colorful tugboat cake (opposite) for dessert.

Nautical Nuggets

SERVES 4 to 6
PREPARATION: 15 minutes
COOKING: 20 minutes

Crunchy, moist, and easy to prepare, these golden morsels are great picnic food.

6 boneless, skinless chicken breast halves
Salt
Freshly ground pepper
1 teaspoon dried oregano
1/2 cup sour cream or plain yogurt
2 tablespoons freshly squeezed lemon juice
1 teaspoon Tabasco
1 garlic clove, finely chopped
2 cups finely crushed saltines or Ritz crackers (about 40 crackers)
1/2 cup sesame seeds
4 tablespoons unsalted butter, melted

■ Remove the filet from each chicken breast and put them in a mixing bowl or container. Cut each chicken breast diagonally into 3 strips and add them to the bowl. Season the chicken generously with salt, pepper, and oregano, rubbing the seasonings into the chicken.

■ Add the sour cream, lemon juice, Tabasco, and garlic to the chicken and turn the pieces until thoroughly coated. Cover the chicken and marinate at room temperature for at least 1 hour, or refrigerate overnight.

■ Preheat oven to 400°F.

■ Spread the saltines and the sesame seeds in a flat dish. Lift the chicken pieces from the marinade one at a time and roll them in the saltine mixture, coating each piece evenly. Arrange the pieces on a lightly oiled baking sheet so that they are barely touching. Drizzle the melted butter over the chicken.

■ Bake the chicken until golden brown and tender, about 20 minutes. Serve hot or at room temperature.

Variation: Substitute pieces of firm fish such as cod, monkfish, or halibut for the chicken.

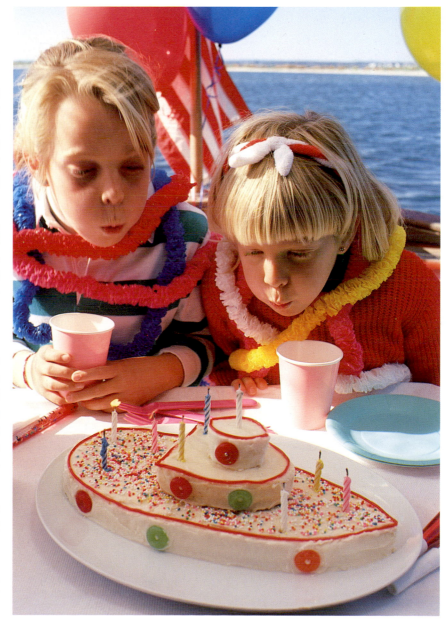

Creamy Potato Salad

SERVES 4 to 6
PREPARATION: 15 minutes
COOKING: 30 minutes

This classic American dish is absolutely delicious. Use potatoes that are approximately the same size, so they will cook evenly.

6 large boiling potatoes (about 1½
*   pounds), scrubbed*
¼ cup white wine vinegar, rice wine
*   vinegar, or cider vinegar*
1 teaspoon Dijon mustard
2 to 3 tablespoons finely chopped onion
1 to 2 teaspoons dried dill
Salt
Freshly ground pepper
½ cup sour cream
½ cup Mayonnaise (page 104)

■ Put the potatoes in a saucepan with cold water to cover. Bring the water to a boil over high heat. Lower the heat and simmer the potatoes until barely tender, about 20 minutes. (When cooked, they will begin to float to the surface.)

■ While the potatoes cook, combine the vinegar, mustard, onion, and dill in a mixing bowl.

■ When potatoes are done, plunge them into cold water for a minute to make handling easier. (Do not leave them in the water, or they will get soggy.) Drain the potatoes, peel them, and cut them into 1-inch chunks. Toss potatoes with the vinegar mixture while still warm, and season to taste with salt and pepper.

■ Make a well in the potato mixture and add the sour cream and mayonnaise, stirring to combine. Incorporate the potatoes into the mayonnaise mixture, folding gently. Keep salad cold until serving.

■ Just before serving, stir the salad gently and adjust the seasoning. Add milk or water to thin the dressing if the salad seems dry.

Vanilla Tugboat Cake

MAKES one 8-inch 2-layer cake
PREPARATION: 15 minutes
COOKING: 30 minutes
ASSEMBLING AND DECORATING: 60 minutes

2 cups all-purpose flour
1 cup sugar
2 teaspoons baking powder
½ teaspoon salt
8 tablespoons (1 stick) unsalted butter,
*   softened*
3 eggs
1 cup milk or sour cream
1 teaspoon vanilla extract

Vanilla Frosting
8 tablespoons (1 stick) unsalted butter,
*   softened*
4 cups confectioners' sugar
1 teaspoon vanilla extract
4 to 6 tablespoons condensed milk

Decoration
Lifesavers
Shoestring licorice
Colored sprinkles

■ Preheat the oven to 350°F. Butter 2 8-inch round layer cake pans, line the bottoms with wax paper, and butter the paper.

■ Combine the flour, sugar, baking powder, and salt in a large mixing bowl. Stir well with a wire whisk. Work in the butter with your fingertips until the mixture resembles coarse meal. Beat the eggs, milk, and vanilla together in a small bowl, then add to the flour mixture and beat until smooth.

■ Pour the battter into the prepared pans. Bake about 30 minutes, or until the top springs back when lightly touched with the fingertips and the edges pull away slightly from the sides of the pan. Let the cakes cool in the pans 10 minutes before turning them out to cool completely on racks.

■ While the cake cools, make the frosting: Beat the butter in a small mixing bowl until creamy. Add the confectioners' sugar gradually, and stir in the vanilla. Beat in a few drops of milk to make the frosting of spreadable consistency.

■ Using a small, sharp knife and one of the cakepans as a guide, make an outline of the front portion of the tugboat in one of the layers. Use the second layer to create the back portion of the boat. Cut out the shapes, trimming them neatly. Form the boat shape, trimming the joining edges to make them fit together neatly. Use the remaining cake to fashion the deckhouse and smokestack.

■ Split the cake for the base layer horizontally and fill with frosting. Frost the sections, then assemble the tugboat, using additional frosting to secure each section. Decorate the boat with Lifesavers and shoestring licorice to simulate portholes and lifelines, pressing the candy gently into the frosting.

Mom's Chocolate Cake
(ALTERNATE RECIPE)

MAKES one 8-inch round cake
PREPARATION: 20 minutes
COOKING: 25 minutes

This simple, easy-to-prepare cake is rich, light, and not too sweet.

8 tablespoons (1 stick) unsalted butter, softened
1 cup sugar
1 egg
3 squares (3 ounces) unsweetened chocolate, melted
1⅓ cups all-purpose flour
1 teaspoon baking powder
1 teaspoon baking soda
½ teaspoon salt
1 cup freshly brewed coffee
1 teaspoon vanilla extract

Chocolate Frosting
MAKES ABOUT 1½ cups
4 tablespoons unsalted butter, softened
1½ cups confectioners' sugar (approximately)
1 teaspoon vanilla extract
1 egg
4 squares (4 ounces) unsweetened chocolate, melted
Coffee or milk

■ Preheat the oven to 350°F. Butter an 8- or 9-inch round layer cake pan.

■ Beat the butter with the sugar in a large mixing bowl until creamy. Add the egg and beat until the mixture is light and fluffy. Stir in the melted chocolate.

■ Combine the dry ingredients and mix well with a whisk. Add the dry ingredients to the butter mixture, alternating with the coffee, and whisk until smooth. Stir in the vanilla. Pour the batter into the prepared pan and bake until a toothpick inserted in the center comes out clean, about 25 minutes. Allow the cake to cool for 10 minutes. Run a knife along the edge of the pan to loosen the cake. Invert the cake on a rack and allow to cool completely. Put on a platter.

■ While the cake cools, make the frosting: Beat the butter in a mixing bowl until creamy. Add 1 cup sugar and mix until smooth. Add the vanilla and egg and beat until smooth. Add the chocolate and stir until smooth, adding more sugar or a few drops of coffee or milk, if necessary, to make the frosting spreadable.

■ When the cake has cooled completely, spread the frosting on the top and side. As an alternative, leave cake in pan and frost only the top. This simplifies storage and transport.

Note: The cake will swell during baking and will emerge with a domed appearance.

"Once in a young lifetime one should be allowed to have as much sweetness as one can possibly want and hold."

Judith Olney

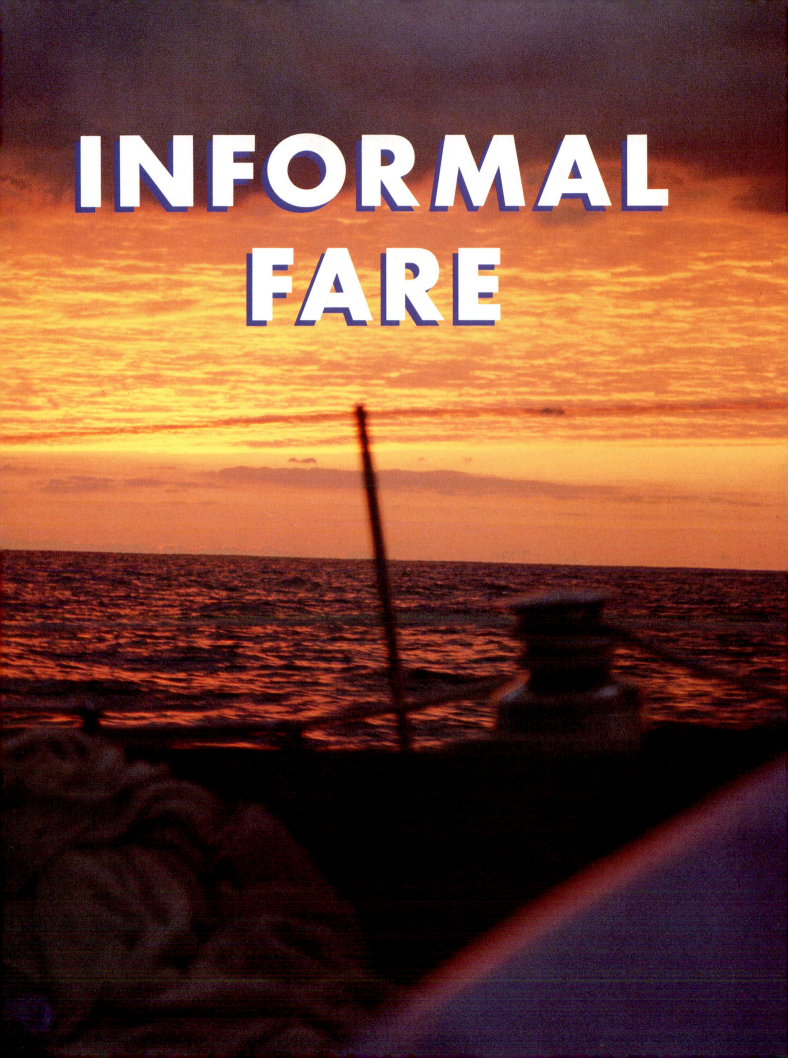

INFORMAL FARE

Breakfast Underway

On overnight passages, after very long evenings spent listening to the flap of a sail or the creak of the boom, sailors come alive at dawn with a renewed sense of vigor. As colors bloom across the horizon, the wet ocean air sharpens the senses. Whether the crew is coming off watch or tumbling out of a warm bunk to the aroma of sizzling sausage and fresh coffee, breakfast is a meal that sailors devour heartily.

Cooking breakfast underway is another story. Merely frying eggs can turn into a comedy routine as the cook tries diligently to hold on to the ingredients, avoid seasickness, and keep balance while the boat pitches and yaws. Pouring orange juice can take an absurd amount of time.

To preserve sanity, new cooking techniques evolve. Steps become consolidated, while Rube Goldbergian devices may be concocted to tame the chaos that erupts when the skipper neglects to inform the cook that the boat is coming about. At sea, priorities change; a wise sea cook will avoid any dish that requires fine mincing or more than two pots.

This does not mean that you cannot eat well at sea. We've enjoyed everything from blueberry pancakes to Western omelets while hundreds of miles offshore. Indeed, to celebrate landfall, Elizabeth once served an elaborate breakfast— complete with scones, fried apples, grits, and sausage—while our boat plowed through 10-foot seas off the coast of St. Thomas. One simply needs to know what to cook and some basic techniques to navigate successfully in the galley under way.

Granola

MAKES ABOUT 14 cups
PREPARATION: 10 minutes
COOKING: 30 minutes

We love this crisp, golden granola for breakfast or as an instant snack to quell a craving for sweets.

2 pounds (8 cups) rolled oats
¾ cup vegetable oil
1 cup maple syrup or honey
½ cup water or apple cider
1 teaspoon salt
1 teaspoon vanilla extract
1 cup nonfat dry milk
2 cups wheat germ
1 cup sesame seeds
1 cup pumpkin seeds
2 cups sliced almonds

■ Preheat the oven to 325°F.

■ Place the oats in a large mixing bowl. Mix the oil, syrup, and water and stir into the oats. Add the salt and vanilla and stir well. Add the remaining ingredients and mix thoroughly. Spread the cereal in a large roasting pan.

■ Bake about 30 minutes, stirring every 5 minutes after the first 10 minutes. Allow the mixture to cool. Store in airtight containers.

Spiced Apple Muffins

MAKES ABOUT 12 large muffins, or one
9 x 5-inch loaf
PREPARATION: 20 minutes
COOKING: 25 minutes (40 minutes for a
loaf)

A tiny amount of cardamom gives the
muffins their delicate spiciness.

½ cup raisins
½ cup currants
½ cup golden rum or dry sherry
*   (optional)*
3 cups all-purpose flour
1 teaspoon salt
1 teaspoon baking soda
1½ cups vegetable oil
2 cups sugar
3 eggs
1 teaspoon cinnamon
1 teaspoon vanilla extract
⅛ teaspoon ground cardamom (see Note)
3 apples, peeled, cored, and cut into
*   ½-inch chunks (about 3 cups)*
1 cup coarsely chopped walnuts or pecans,
*   or slivered almonds (optional)*

■ If desired, combine the raisins, currants, and rum in a small bowl and set
aside to steep for 1 hour or overnight.

■ Preheat the oven to 350°F. Place
paper liners in 12 muffin cups, or butter
a 9 x 5-inch loaf pan and line the bottom
with wax paper.

■ Combine the flour, salt, and baking
soda, mix well with a wire whisk, and set
aside.

■ Beat the oil and sugar with a wire
whisk. Add the eggs, cinnamon, vanilla,
and cardamom and beat until the mixture
is smooth and creamy. Stir in the dry ingredients. Gently fold in the apples, nuts,
and raisin-rum mixture. Spoon the batter
into prepared muffin cups or loaf pan.

■ Bake until well risen and browned
and a toothpick inserted in the center of
a muffin comes out clean, about 25 minutes (40 minutes for a loaf).

Note: If you do not have cardamom,
substitute an equal amount of cloves or
ginger.

Buttermilk Bran Muffins

MAKES ABOUT 15 muffins
PREPARATION: 20 minutes
COOKING: 20 minutes

The batter for these husky muffins can
be kept refrigerated for up to 1 month.

2 cups bran cereal, such as All-Bran
½ cup wheat or oat bran
¾ cup currants or raisins
½ teaspoon salt
1 cup boiling water
¾ cup brown sugar
2 eggs
1 cup buttermilk
⅓ cup vegetable oil
1 cup unbleached all-purpose flour
½ cup whole wheat flour
2 teaspoons baking soda

■ Combine the cereal, bran, currants,
and salt in a large mixing bowl. Pour the
boiling water over the mixture and set
aside. When the mixture is cool, add the
sugar, eggs, buttermilk, and oil and mix
well.

■ In a separate medium bowl, combine the flours and baking soda with a
wire whisk. Stir the dry ingredients into
the liquid ingredients and mix well.

■ Store the batter in airtight containers and refrigerate up to 1 month.

■ When ready to bake, preheat the
oven to 375°F. Spoon the batter into
paper-lined muffin tins. Bake until well
risen and browned and a toothpick inserted into the center of a muffin comes
out clean, about 20 minutes. Serve hot
with cream cheese or butter and your favorite jam.

Variation: Add grated raw carrot,
diced apple, chopped nuts, or grated orange rind to the batter just before baking.

**MAKING
OATMEAL**
■

Late at night, prepare
oatmeal for an early
morning watch by com-
bining old-fashioned oats
with boiling water in a
wide-mouthed Thermos.
Cap the Thermos, and
after a few hours, the oats
will be cooked and hot
for a comforting break-
fast. Follow the direc-
tions on the oatmeal box
for proportions, bearing
in mind that instant or
quick-coooking oats re-
quire far less time and
will be mushy if left overnight.

THE *EMILY*

■

The well-designed galley of *Emily* (right), owned by a Connecticut racing family, is a joy to use. Thoughtful features include:

· A U-shaped layout, enabling the cook to wedge in firmly during rough weather.

· A location near the companionway, allowing good ventilation and easy access to both cabin table and cockpit. (In a pinch, the cook can even tail the genoa sheets!)

· A stainless-steel sink deep enough to hold plates that are soaking in soapy water.

· A second sink for rinsing dishes or storing food, bottles, and mugs in rough weather.

· Foot-operated fresh and seawater faucets.

· A paper towel holder near the companionway (handy for spills and rain-splattered spectacles).

· A safety harness and padded bar across the front of the stove.

· Fiddle rails on the stovetop and raised rims on the counters.

· Two foldup counters near the sink.

· A secure, recessed knife holder.

· Two waste receptacles (for garbage and trash).

· Clear lucite dividers in the refrigerator, with holes for ventilation.

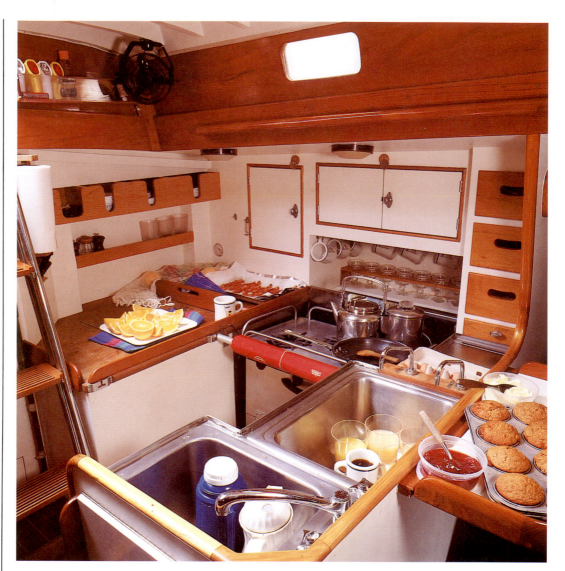

Scrambled Eggs Under-way

SERVES 3 to 4
PREPARATION: 5 minutes
COOKING: 10 minutes

This elemental recipe for scrambled eggs can be embellished as predilections and circumstances allow.

4 tablespoons (½ stick) unsalted butter
8 eggs
Salt
Freshly ground pepper or Tabasco

■ Melt the butter in a medium saucepan over medium heat. Remove the pan from the heat and break the eggs into the pan.

■ Return the pan to the heat and stir the eggs gently, regulating the speed at which they cook by moving the pan on and off the heat. For soft, finely textured eggs, cook slowly, stirring with a slow, constant motion. For larger, drier curds, allow the eggs to congeal slightly on the bottom of the pan before stirring to allow the uncooked egg to flow underneath. Season with salt and pepper to taste just before the eggs are done.

Note: If you want to add grated cheese to the eggs, stir it in just before the eggs are cooked and allow it to melt. Cream cheese can be added at the beginning of the cooking because its high fat content allows it to blend creamily into the eggs. Other add-in options include: cooked ham, sausage, or bacon; a little mustard; chopped herbs; tomato sauce; sautéed mushrooms; and stir-fried broccoli.

"Don't fry bacon in your birthday suit."
Circumnavigators Mimi and Dan Dyer

French Toast

SERVES 3 to 4
PREPARATION: 10 minutes
COOKING: 15 minutes

To make good French Toast, use thick slices of slightly stale bread. We often use French or Italian bread left over from a previous meal.

3 eggs
¾ cup milk or evaporated milk
1 tablespoon sugar
1 teaspoon vanilla extract
¼ teaspoon grated lemon rind (optional)
Freshly grated nutmeg
½ teaspoon cinnamon
2 tablespoons rum (optional)
6 slices bread
Unsalted butter

■ Mix together all the ingredients except the bread in a wide container deep enough to prevent the egg mixture from spilling in a bouncy seaway. Whisk the mixture well.

■ Add the bread to the mixture and soak about 15 minutes, turning the pieces to make sure they absorb the egg mixture evenly. (Drier bread may require longer soaking.)

■ Heat a large skillet over medium heat and add enough butter to coat the bottom of the pan. Lift the bread slices from the egg mixture and slip them into the pan. Fry gently about 5 minutes on each side, or until crusty and golden brown. Serve the French Toast immediately with syrup, jam, yogurt, sautéed apples, or warm applesauce.

Note: The rule of thumb for proportioning eggs to milk for French Toast is ¼ cup milk to 1 large egg. If convenient, soak the bread in the egg mixture overnight in an airtight container in the refrigerator.

Variation: Sandwich cream cheese between two slices of cinnamon-raisin bread before soaking as described in the egg mixture.

Whole Wheat Pancakes

SERVES 4 to 6
PREPARATION: 15 minutes
COOKING: 10 minutes

Serve these classic flapjacks hot off the griddle.

2 cups whole wheat flour
1 cup all-purpose flour
½ teaspoon salt
2 teaspoons baking powder
¼ cup brown sugar
3 large eggs
6 tablespoons melted unsalted butter or vegetable oil
3 cups milk (or a mixture of milk and sour cream or plain yogurt)
Vegetable oil

■ Mix the flours, salt, baking powder, and sugar in a mixing bowl. Make a well in the center of the dry ingredients and break the eggs into it. Beat the eggs with a fork without incorporating the dry ingredients, until the whites and yolks are combined. Add the butter and milk, then stir the dry ingredients into the liquid until just moistened.

■ Heat a griddle or large skillet over moderate heat until a drop of water evaporates instantly from the surface of the pan. Brush the pan with oil and wipe away the excess with a paper towel. (If you favor pancakes with crunchy edges, leave the extra oil in the pan and replenish as you go along.)

■ Drop spoonfuls of batter onto the griddle and cook about 2 minutes, or until the edges are dry and bubbles appear on the surface. Flip the pancakes and cook 2 minutes longer. Serve immediately.

Notes: If you like fluffy pancakes, separate the eggs and beat the whites until stiff. Beat the yolks with the butter and milk and stir just until the dry ingredients are blended; then fold in the whites.

If no fresh milk is available, canned milk or cartons of Longlife milk work well. Or, mix an equal proportion of sour cream or plain yogurt with water or orange juice. Or add ½ cup nonfat dry milk to the dry ingredients and substitute water or juice for the liquid.

Baked Puffed Pancake

SERVES 4
PREPARATION: 15 minutes
COOKING: 30 minutes

Serve this gloriously puffy pancake with fried apples and cottage cheese or sautéed bananas with lime.

*¼ cup vegetable oil or melted unsalted
    butter*
4 eggs
1 cup all-purpose flour
1 cup milk or evaporated milk
1 teaspoon vanilla extract

■ Preheat the oven to 425°F. Pour 1 tablespoon oil into a large skillet and place it in the oven to heat while making the batter.

■ Break the eggs into a mixing bowl and beat them with a whisk until blended. Add the flour and whisk to combine. Add the milk, vanilla, and remaining oil and beat until smooth.

■ Remove the skillet from the oven and pour in the batter, which should sizzle ferociously. If it doesn't, your pan is not hot enough, and you will have a less puffy pancake.

■ Bake the pancake without disturbing until it rises, billowing from the pan, about 25 minutes. Serve at once, cut into wedges.

Note: Without the vanilla, this is Yorkshire pudding, or popovers if baked in individual cups.

Corn Pancakes

SERVES 4 to 6
PREPARATION: 10 minutes
COOKING: 20 minutes

Stud your cakes with fresh raspberries or blueberries for a special treat.

1 cup all-purpose flour
½ cup white or yellow cornmeal
1 tablespoon sugar
2 teaspoons baking powder
1 teaspoon salt
3 eggs
*2 tablespoons melted unsalted butter or
    vegetable oil*
¾ cup milk
*1 cup fresh corn kernels, or 1 8-ounce can
    cream-style corn*
Vegetable oil

■ Mix the dry ingredients in a large mixing bowl. Make a well in the center and break the eggs into it. Beat the eggs with a fork until the whites and yolks are combined, taking care not to incorporate the dry ingredients more than necessary. Add the butter, then add the milk slowly, stirring the dry ingredients into the liquid until just moistened. Stir in the corn.

■ Heat a griddle or large skillet over medium heat until a drop of water evaporates instantly from the surface. Brush the pan with oil, and wipe off the excess with a paper towel. (If you favor pancakes with crunchy edges, leave the extra oil in the pan and replenish as necessary.)

■ Drop spoonfuls of the batter onto the griddle and cook until the pancake edges are dry and bubbles appear in the center, about 2 minutes. Flip the pancakes and cook 2 minutes longer. Serve immediately.

Note: Don't confine this dish to breakfast. Serve tiny corn pancakes for dinner along with a simple roast or with creamed chicken.

FAST TACKS
■

· To prevent spills, make sure pots and equipment are secure at all times.

· Don't fill pots more than halfway.

· Set glasses and mugs in the sink when pouring liquids into them.

· Keep the sink clear so that it can be used to hold bowls of pancake batter, milk containers, cooking equipment, etc.

· Set pots on folded damp towels to help prevent pots from sliding.

· Use a Thermos to keep beverages hot. Fill one with boiling water for tea, instant coffee, soup, hot chocolate mix, etc.

· Make pans serve double duty; mix and cook scrambled eggs in one pan, etc.

· Chop herbs with scissors into a glass or mug. Crush walnuts, crackers, etc. in plastic bags using a heavy bottle.

· Didactic as it may sound, clean up as you go along.

Sailor's Rum Syrup

MAKES ABOUT 2 cups
PREPARATION: 5 minutes
COOKING: 10 minutes

This rich rum syrup was created somewhere between Southwest Harbor, Maine, and St. George's, Bermuda, when the passion for pancakes outstripped the maple syrup supply.

1½ cups brown or white sugar
6 tablespoons water or juice
1 small cinnamon stick (optional)
2 whole cloves or whole allspice (optional)
2 or 3 slices of lime, lemon, or orange (optional)
4 to 6 tablespoons light or dark rum

■ Place all the ingredients except the rum in a saucepan. Bring the mixture to a boil, stirring from time to time. Lower the heat and simmer until the syrup has thickened, about 10 minutes.

■ Allow the syrup to cool. Remove the whole spices and fruit. Stir in the rum and mix until smooth.

Fried Apples

SERVES 4
PREPARATION: 10 minutes
COOKING: 15 minutes

Fried apples are incredibly simple to prepare. For a wonderful dessert, serve them hot with a dollop of yogurt or whipped cream.

4 apples, such as winesap or macoun, peeled, quartered, and cored
4 tablespoons (½ stick) unsalted butter
3 to 4 tablespoons sugar
Cinnamon

■ Cut the apples into thick slices.

■ Heat the butter in a skillet over medium heat. When the butter foams, add the apples in one layer. Cook, turning the slices gently, until they begin to brown slightly. Sprinkle the apples with the sugar and cinnamon and continue to cook until the sugar melts and caramelizes. Serve immediately.

Note: Some apples, especially old ones, may disintegrate into mush as they are cooked. If this happens, simply stir the apples into a rough sauce, add a little seasoning—maybe some rum or Cognac as well as the cinnamon—and serve them anyway.

Grilled Breakfast Sandwich

SERVES 4
PREPARATION: 10 minutes
COOKING: 10 minutes

One gray morning, after a rough night off the coast of North Carolina, Elizabeth passed these hot sandwiches, wrapped in paper towels, topside to restore the weary crew.

3 eggs
¾ cup evaporated milk
Tabasco
Worcestershire sauce
Crumbled dried herbs such as oregano, thyme, or herbes de Provence
8 slices bread
Thinly sliced cooked ham
Thinly sliced cheese such as Cheddar or Swiss
Mustard
Vegetable oil

■ Beat the eggs with the milk in a high-sided container such as a roasting pan, adding seasonings and herbs to taste.

■ Make sandwiches with the bread, ham, and cheese, brushing mustard on the insides of the bread.

■ Carefully immerse the sandwiches in the egg mixture, and soak them 2 to 3 minutes.

■ Heat a large skillet over medium heat, lightly oil it, and carefully slip the sandwiches into the pan. Fry until the cheese melts and the bread is golden on both sides.

"Raib appears in the doorway of the deckhouse and gazes balefully to windward. The sea, roiled suddenly by squall, turns a soft black. Soon rain is pelting on the deckhouse roof, running off in wind-shaped strings. Raib cups it in his hand and splashes it in his face, then drinks some, gasping.

'I tell you, Vemon, to drink fresh rain dat way is something good.'"

Peter Matthiessen,
Far Tortuga

Easy Midday Salads

On a beautiful summer day, when few of us feel like spending time in the galley, cool salads are a wonderful foil to the midday heat and humidity. Quick to prepare, they also invite the creative use of last night's leftovers. The secrets of their success are to keep them simple, to use the freshest ingredients available, and to take a few extra minutes to arrange them attractively. Although the following salads are ideal for light lunches, we've also been known to serve them on hot summer nights, expanding the meal with complementary salads, bread, and dessert.

Marinated Steak Salad

SERVES 4 to 6
PREPARATION: 20 minutes
COOKING: About 15 minutes

You can add a jar of marinated artichoke hearts (our favorite instant ingredient) to this salad, with good effect.

2 pounds sirloin steak, or top round or
*   flank steak*
Salt
Freshly ground pepper
1 large red onion, thinly sliced, or 1
*   bunch scallions, thinly sliced*
2 or 3 firm ripe tomatoes, cut into wedges
½ cup chopped fresh parsley

Dressing
1 to 2 teaspoons anchovy paste, or 2
*   anchovies, rinsed and finely chopped*
1 garlic clove, pressed or finely chopped
1 tablespoon Dijon mustard
3 to 4 tablespoons red wine vinegar
½ cup olive oil or vegetable oil
Salt
Freshly ground pepper

■ Prepare the grill (page 13).

■ Rub the steak with salt and a generous amount of pepper. Cook the steak on a grill or pan broil it in a heavy skillet, about 8 minutes per side, keeping it rare. Allow the steak to cool and cut it across the grain into ¼-inch slices. Cut the slices into 1½-inch lengths and place them in a large mixing bowl. Add the onion, tomatoes, and parsley.

■ Put the dressing ingredients into a container with a tight-fitting lid. Shake vigorously, and pour the dressing over the ingredients in the bowl. Toss lightly. Serve the salad on a platter or on individual plates.

Variations: Make a steak sandwich by tucking the salad into French bread or hard rolls.

Or expand the salad into a main course with freshly boiled potatoes: Cook the potatoes until tender, cool them slightly, then peel them and toss them with some of the dressing. Add the potatoes to the steak salad or serve them alongside.

Suggested Wine: Zinfandel or Hermitage.

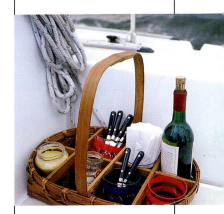

Compartmentalized basket neatly holds glasses and cutlery steady at sea.

Marinated Zucchini Salad

SERVES 4 to 6
PREPARATION: 15 minutes
COOKING: 10 minutes

This colorful vinegar-splashed salad mellows as it sits. It is a piquant accompaniment to grilled pork, chicken, or fish.

6 medium zucchini
½ cup olive oil
Salt
1 small onion, sliced
2 garlic cloves, finely chopped
1 cup chopped, peeled, and seeded ripe fresh tomatoes or canned tomatoes
1 teaspoon sugar
¼ cup red wine vinegar

■ Slice the zucchini at an angle into ¼-inch-thick ovals.

■ Heat the oil in a large skillet over medium-high heat. Cook the zucchini slices, tossing occasionally, until tender but still crisp, about 10 minutes. Remove the slices to a shallow dish, spreading the pieces so that they do not steam and become soggy. Season to taste with salt. Lower the heat to medium.

■ Add the onion and garlic to the pan and cook, stirring, until softened, about 5 minutes. Add the tomatoes and cook until the mixture is thick. Add the sugar and vinegar and cook 1 minute. Pour the sauce over the zucchini and toss gently. Serve hot or at room temperature.

Sprout Salad

SERVES 4 to 6
PREPARATION: 15 minutes

Dressing
1 teaspoon Dijon mustard
1 teaspoon dried dill
3 tablespoons freshly squeezed lemon juice
¼ cup vegetable oil
Salt
Freshly ground pepper

Salad
1 quart alfalfa, lentil, or mung bean sprouts, or a mixture
2 or 3 sliced scallions, or ¼ cup finely chopped onion
2 carrots, grated
1 cucumber, peeled, seeded, and chopped

■ Combine the ingredients for the dressing in a salad bowl, whisk well, and adjust the seasoning to taste. Add the sprouts, scallions, carrots, and cucumber and toss well. Serve immediately.

White Bean Salad with Tuna

SERVES 4 to 6
PREPARATION: 10 minutes

Though canned white beans and tuna are dull on their own, they can be transformed into a filling and robust salad when dressed with olive oil and vinegar and seasoned with herbs. Taken a step further, this salad is sensational made with grilled tuna steaks and freshly cooked beans, tossed with virgin olive oil.

2 6½-ounce cans light tuna, drained
Salt
Freshly ground pepper
Garlic Vinaigrette (page 77)
2 15-ounce cans white cannellini beans, drained
½ cup chopped red onion
1 or 2 ripe tomatoes (optional)

■ Break the tuna into large chunks in a mixing bowl, season to taste with salt and pepper, and add half the vinaigrette. Toss gently and set aside to marinate 10 minutes. Add the beans, onion, and remaining vinaigrette, and toss again.

■ When ready to serve, cut the tomatoes into wedges or chunks and arrange them around the salad.

Note: For piquancy, add 1 or 2 pinches crushed red pepper to the vinaigrette.

Suggested Wine: A crisp white such as Sauvignon Blanc.

Rice Salad with Shrimp, Feta Cheese, and Dill

SERVES 4 to 6
PREPARATION: 20 minutes
COOKING: 30 minutes

This pretty salad makes a hearty main course that can be embellished with sliced hard-cooked eggs, wedges of juicy tomatoes, slivers of ham, or chunks of cucumber.

3 tablespoons olive oil
2 cups uncooked long-grain white rice
1 small bay leaf
3¾ cups water
¼ cup freshly squeezed lemon juice, white wine vinegar, or rice wine vinegar
1 tablespoon dried dill, or 4 to 5 tablespoons chopped fresh dill
1 garlic clove, finely chopped
Salt
Freshly ground pepper
1 bunch scallions, finely sliced
1 red bell pepper, stemmed, seeded, and thinly sliced
½ cup olives (optional)
1 cup crumbled feta cheese
2 cups cooked, peeled, and deveined shrimp

■ Heat the oil in a large, heavy saucepan over medium heat. Add the rice and bay leaf and cook, stirring, until the grains begin to turn white. Add the water and raise the heat to high. Bring the liquid to a boil. Cover the pot tightly, reduce the heat to low, and cook undisturbed for 20 minutes.

■ While the rice is cooking, combine the lemon juice, dill, and garlic in a large nonreactive mixing bowl.

■ Remove the rice from the heat and allow it to stand, covered, 10 minutes more. Turn the rice into the mixing bowl. Fluff the grains with a fork and toss lightly with the lemon juice mixture. Season to taste with salt and pepper. Set the rice aside to cool, tossing occasionally.

■ Fold the scallions, pepper, olives, and half the cheese and shrimp into the rice. Taste the salad and correct the seasoning. Place the salad in a serving dish, top with the remaining cheese and shrimp, and garnish with a few olives if desired.

Note: To keep the rice grains separate and fluffy, resist the temptation to lift the cover or stir the rice while it cooks.

Suggested Wine: A simple, light wine such as white Zinfandel, or a robust red wine such as Cabernet or Barbera.

Tuna and Artichoke Heart Salad

MAKES ABOUT 3 cups
PREPARATION: 15 minutes

This quickly made salad is delicious with a baguette or tucked inside a pita pocket.

2 6½-ounce cans light tuna, drained
Lemon juice
1 teaspoon dried oregano
Freshly ground pepper
1 6½-ounce jar marinated artichoke hearts, drained
2 tablespoons finely chopped onion
2 tablespoons finely chopped fresh parsley
½ cup mayonnaise

■ In a mixing bowl, break the tuna into large flakes with a fork. Sprinkle the tuna with lemon juice, oregano, and pepper to taste. Toss mixture lightly.

■ Cut the artichoke hearts into ¼-inch slices and add them to the tuna. Stir in the onion and parsley and toss. Fold in the mayonnaise and taste for seasoning.

Variations: Spoon the salad onto a slice of bread, cover with cheese, and heat under the broiler until the cheese melts.

Or omit the mayonnaise and add a can of drained white or red kidney beans. Season with oil and vinegar, and add chopped onion, olives, and celery.

CHOPPED DELIGHTS

■

Raw vegetable salads are ideally suited to boating because they are uncomplicated and refreshing. Some possibilities:

· Grated turnips tossed with dill, lemon juice, and cream.

· Grated carrots and radishes tossed with sliced scallions and dressed with olive oil and lemon juice.

· Avocado, grapefruit, and red onions sprinkled with vinegar or lime juice.

· Thinly sliced zucchini and other summer squash marinated in vinaigrette and sprinkled with finely chopped scallion.

· Thinly sliced cucumbers, bell peppers, and red onion tossed with dill.

Cool cottage cheese and vegetable salad with crisp rye crackers.

Pretty pickled beet and onion salad with shrimp.

Robust marinated steak salad.

An Italian white bean salad with tuna.

Beet and Pickled Onion Salad

SERVES 4 to 6
PREPARATION: 15 minutes

This tart, bright salad goes well with pickled herring or cold roasted meats, especially pork. Place a dollop of sour cream or plain yogurt on each plate to mix into the salad. Toast the walnuts to intensify their flavor and make them extra crunchy.

1 pound sliced cooked beets
3 tablespoons marinade from Pickled Red
  Onions (recipe follows)
6 tablespoons vegetable oil
Salt
Freshly ground pepper
¼ cup Pickled Red Onions (recipe
  follows)
¼ cup coarsely chopped walnuts

■ Drain the beets and put them in a large mixing bowl. Add the marinade and oil, toss well, and set aside for at least 15 minutes. Season to taste with salt and pepper.

■ To serve, arrange the beets attractively on a serving dish. Scatter the onions on top, and sprinkle with walnuts.

Variation: Toss a green apple sliced into thin wedges and a freshly steamed potato cut into rounds into the salad.

Pickled Red Onions

MAKES ABOUT 2 cups
PREPARATION: 10 minutes

2 medium red onions, peeled and cut into
  ⅛-inch wedges or rings
¼ cup cider vinegar or red wine vinegar
¼ cup water
1 teaspoon salt
½ teaspoon dried oregano
1 teaspoon crushed red pepper

■ Put the onions in a large bowl and cover with boiling water. Allow the onions to soak 5 minutes, then drain.

■ Place the drained onions in a glass container with a tight-sealing lid. Add the remaining ingredients and set aside to marinate at least 1 hour. The onions will keep, refrigerated, for at least 1 week.

Stir-Fried Broccoli Salad

SERVES 4 to 6
PREPARATION: 15 minutes
COOKING: 10 minutes

This pretty emerald green salad is tart and crunchy.

1 large head broccoli
3 tablespoons vegetable oil
1 garlic clove, unpeeled and lightly
  crushed
1 tablespoon sugar
2 tablespoons soy sauce
2 tablespoons red wine vinegar or cider
  vinegar
1 teaspoon sesame oil (optional)
Sesame seeds (optional)
Peanuts, walnuts, or pecans (optional)
Grated orange or lemon rind (optional)

■ Cut the broccoli into flowerets. Reserve the top 4 inches of the stem and cut it into ½-inch pieces.

■ Heat the oil in a large, heavy skillet with a tight-fitting lid over high heat. Add the broccoli stems and garlic and stir-fry 30 seconds. Add the flowerets and stir-fry about 1 minute, until the flowerets turn a brilliant green. Sprinkle with sugar. Add about 3 tablespoons water and cover the pan. Cook until the flowerets are just tender, about 2 minutes. Remove the cover and cook until the moisture has evaporated and the broccoli begins to sizzle. Add the soy sauce, vinegar, and sesame oil, stir quickly, and turn the broccoli into a serving dish. Discard the garlic. Serve warm or cold, sprinkled with sesame seeds or nuts. For variety, toss in a teaspoon of grated orange or lemon rind.

Note: This salad goes well with black bean soup, any grilling menu, or the White Bean Salad with Tuna (page 124).

THE BEET GOES ON...

■

A wonderful way to cook fresh beets is by roasting them. Cut off the greens, leaving the long taproot intact. Wrap the beets in aluminum foil and cook in a 350°F. oven 45 to 60 minutes, or until the beets yield to a skewer poked through the foil. When cool, the skins will slip off easily. The intense earthy flavor of beets prepared in this way will convert you forever.

Cottage Cheese and Vegetable Salad

SERVES 4 to 6
PREPARATION: 20 minutes

This versatile salad is good with crisp rye crackers or as a dip with raw vegetables. For a cool, light lunch, serve it with sliced ripe tomatoes, cucumbers, and a few olives.

1 pound large-curd cottage cheese
2 scallions, finely sliced
4 to 5 radishes, chopped
1 small green bell pepper, stemmed, seeded, and chopped
1 cucumber, peeled, seeded, and chopped
1 tablespoon dried dill, or 2 to 3 tablespoons chopped fresh dill
1/4 cup sour cream
1/4 cup mayonnaise
Salt to taste
Freshly ground pepper to taste

■ Drain the cottage cheese in a fine sieve about 20 minutes. Turn the cheese into a large mixing bowl and add the remaining ingredients. Taste and adjust seasoning. Keep cold until ready to serve.

Variation: Add a handful of crumbled feta cheese to the salad, drizzle with a little olive oil, and top with a sprinkling of fresh chopped herbs.

Marinated Chick-Pea Salad

SERVES 4 to 6
PREPARATION: 15 minutes plus 30 minutes marinating

1 1-pound can chick-peas, drained
3 tablespoons finely chopped red or yellow onion
1 celery stalk, chopped
1 red or green bell pepper, cored and finely sliced
2 teaspoons herbes de Provence, or a mixture of thyme, oregano, and rosemary
3 tablespoons red wine vinegar

1/3 cup olive oil
Salt
Freshly ground pepper

■ Combine the ingredients in a mixing bowl and season to taste with salt and pepper. Marinate at least 2 hours before serving. The salad will keep in the refrigerator up to 1 week.

Variation: Instead of chick-peas, use red beans, white beans, pinto beans, or a combination. Embellish with hard-boiled eggs, tomatoes, cucumbers, tuna, or cold roast chicken.

Smoked Chicken Salad with Dates and Pecans

SERVES 4
PREPARATION: 20 minutes

Smoked meats go naturally with fruity flavors.

3 cups diced smoked boneless chicken or turkey
1 celery stalk, thinly sliced
1 or 2 scallions, finely sliced
1/3 cup mango chutney
2 tablespoons white wine vinegar or apple cider vinegar
1 teaspoon curry powder
1/3 cup vegetable oil
1 apple, cored and thinly sliced
5 or 6 large dates, pitted and sliced lengthwise into strips
1/2 cup pecan halves

■ Place the chicken, celery, and scallions in a large mixing bowl. Combine the chutney, vinegar, and curry in a small bowl. Whisk in the oil. Pour the dressing over the chicken and toss lightly. Add the apples, dates, and pecans and toss lightly again.

Variation: For a richer, creamy salad, substitute a mixture of 1/2 cup mayonnaise and 1/2 cup sour cream for the oil and add more curry to taste.

Suggested Wine: A dry, earthy white such as a Rhône.

Potato and Vegetable Salad

SERVES 4 to 6
PREPARATION: 20 minutes
COOKING: 20 minutes

This substantial salad has satisfying textures and pretty, muted colors. It can easily be expanded into a full meal by adding sliced cold roast lamb, crumbled feta or cubed mozzarella cheese, tomato wedges, or hard-boiled eggs.

*1 pound small red potatoes, cut into
  quarters*
*½ pound carrots, peeled and cut
  diagonally into 2-inch lengths*
*½ pound green beans, cut into 2-inch
  lengths*
½ cup dry white wine
*3 tablespoons finely chopped red or yellow
  onion*
½ cup olive oil
*2 or 3 tablespoons white wine vinegar
Salt
Freshly ground pepper
2 6½-ounce jars marinated artichoke
  hearts, drained
½ cup oil-cured black olives (optional)
3 to 4 tablespoons chopped fresh parsley
  and/or basil*

■ Steam the potatoes, carrots, and green beans separately until tender. As they are cooked, turn them into a large mixing bowl and tumble gently with the wine. Stir in the onion. Sprinkle with the oil and vinegar and season to taste with salt and pepper. Turn the vegetables in the marinade as they cool.

■ Scatter the artichoke hearts and olives on the vegetables and sprinkle with the onion and parsley or basil. Toss the salad gently and serve.

Suggested Wine: A light dry white such as Pinot Bianco.

Tea at Sea

Whether on land or at sea, Australian and British sailors enjoy the custom of afternoon tea. We've adopted this civilized tradition on the high seas and encourage you to do so, too. The following sweets are perfect for teatime treats, not to mention night watches and evening desserts.

Applesauce Cake

MAKES one 8-inch cake
PREPARATION: 30 minutes
COOKING: 25 minutes

> 8 tablespoons (1 stick) unsalted butter, softened
> ¾ cup brown sugar
> 1 egg
> 1 teaspoon vanilla extract
> 1 cup chunky applesauce
> 2 cups all-purpose flour
> 1 teaspoon baking soda
> 1 teaspoon cinnamon
> ½ teaspoon ground cloves
> ½ teaspoon freshly grated nutmeg
> 1 cup chopped raisins or dates
> ½ cup coarsely chopped pecans, walnuts, or sliced almonds

Sugar Glaze
1 cup confectioners' sugar
2 tablespoons lemon juice
1 tablespoon rum or brandy

■ Preheat the oven to 325°F. Butter an 8-inch round layer cake pan and dust the inside with flour.

■ In a mixing bowl, beat the butter with a wooden spoon until creamy. Add the brown sugar gradually, beating until the mixture is smooth and light. Add the egg and beat until smooth. Stir in the vanilla and the applesauce.

■ Put the flour, baking soda, cinnamon, cloves, and nutmeg in a mixing bowl and stir with a whisk to blend. Stir the dry ingredients into the applesauce mixture until no streaks of flour are visible. Fold in the raisins and the nuts. Turn the mixture into the prepared pan.

■ Bake in the oven about 25 minutes, or until the cake pulls away from the sides of the pan and a toothpick inserted in the center comes out clean. Allow the cake to cool in the pan for 10 minutes before turning it out on a rack.

■ Combine the confectioners' sugar, lemon juice, and rum for the glaze and stir until the mixture is smooth. Spoon the glaze over the top of the warm cake.

Orange Cake

MAKES two 9 x 5-inch loaves
PREPARATION: 30 minutes
COOKING: 50 minutes

Freshly brewed tea or coffee is delicious with this moist sweet cake.

2 cups all-purpose flour
1 teaspoon baking powder
1 teaspoon baking soda
½ teaspoon salt
8 tablespoons (1 stick) unsalted butter,
  softened
1 cup sugar
3 eggs
1 teaspoon vanilla extract
Grated rind of 1 orange or lemon
1 cup sour cream or plain yogurt
¼ cup orange liqueur, such as Cointreau
  or Grand Marnier
1 cup coarsely chopped walnuts or pecans

Glaze
½ cup sugar
½ cup orange juice
⅓ cup orange liqueur

■ Preheat the oven to 325°F. Butter the 9 x 5-inch loaf pans.

■ Place the flour, baking powder, baking soda, and salt in a medium mixing bowl and combine with a whisk.

■ Beat the butter in a large mixing bowl until creamy. Gradually add the sugar, beating until the mixture is light. Add the eggs 1 at a time, beating the mixture until smooth after each addition. Add the vanilla and orange rind. Mix the sour cream with the orange liqueur and stir into the butter mixture alternately with the dry mixture. Fold in the nuts. Divide the mixture evenly between the 2 pans. Rap the pans sharply on the counter to settle the batter.

■ Bake the loaves 50 minutes, or until a toothpick inserted in the center comes out clean.

■ While the cakes are baking, mix together the sugar, orange juice, and orange liqueur for the glaze in a bowl.

■ Turn the loaves out onto a rack set over a pan and allow to cool for 10 minutes. Using a skewer or ice pick, prick the top of each loaf at ½-inch intervals.

■ Spoon or brush the glaze over the loaves while they are still warm, waiting until the liquid has been absorbed before applying more. When the loaves are cool, wrap them well in foil.

Lemon Bars

MAKES 16 2-inch bars
PREPARATION: 30 minutes
COOKING: 30 minutes

A classic American sweet that Elizabeth was fond of in childhood.

1 cup all-purpose flour
¼ cup confectioners' sugar
8 tablespoons (1 stick) unsalted butter
3 eggs
1 cup sugar
½ cup freshly squeezed lemon or lime
  juice (about 3 lemons or 4 limes)
Grated rind of lemon or lime
Confectioners' sugar, for dusting

■ Preheat the oven to 350°F. Butter an 8 x 8 baking pan.

■ Mix the flour and the confectioners' sugar in a bowl. Cut the butter into thin slices and work it into the dry ingredients with your fingertips until the mixture resembles coarse crumbs. Pat the mixture evenly into the bottom and ¾ inch up the sides of the prepared pan.

■ Bake until the pastry is pale gold, about 15 minutes.

■ In the same bowl, whisk the eggs lightly. Gradually whisk in the sugar, and beat until thick. Beat in the lemon juice and rind. Pour the mixture onto the baked pastry and return the pan to the oven.

■ Bake until the filling is set, about 15 minutes. When cool, sprinkle with confectioners' sugar and cut into 2-inch bars.

"It's just past 3 in the P.M. So far my intake consists of:

2 bowls Cocoa Krispies
1 bowl Sugar Pops
1 Lite Beer (at 11 A.M.)
3 helpings of Liz's (fantastic) hot sesame noodles
5 buttered crackers
1 Goo Goo Cluster
3 of Liz's (incredible) chocolate-chip cookies

By the time I get home I'll look like Jabba the Hutt."

From the diary of Christopher Buckley, on a trans-Pacific passage aboard Sealestial

Banana Bread

MAKES one 9 x 5-inch loaf
PREPARATION: 30 minutes
COOKING: 45 minutes

> 8 tablespoons (1 stick) unsalted butter,
>   softened
> 1 cup brown sugar
> 2 eggs
> 1 teaspoon vanilla extract
> 1/4 teaspoon freshly grated nutmeg
> 3 very ripe bananas, peeled and mashed
> 2 cups all-purpose flour
> 1 teaspoon baking soda
> 1/2 teaspoon baking powder
> 1/2 teaspoon salt
> 1/2 cup coarsely chopped walnuts or pecans
> 1 tablespoon chopped candied ginger

■ Preheat the oven to 350°F. Butter a 9 x 5-inch loaf pan.

■ Beat the butter and sugar in a mixing bowl until creamy. Add the eggs 1 at a time, beating well after each addition. Stir in the vanilla, nutmeg, and bananas.

■ Mix the dry ingredients well with a whisk and add them to the banana mixture, stirring just until the batter is smooth. Fold in the nuts and ginger. Turn the mixture into the pan and bake until a toothpick inserted in the middle comes out clean, about 45 minutes.

Peanut Butter Cookies

MAKES ABOUT 40 cookies
PREPARATION: 20 minutes
COOKING: 10 to 12 minutes

> 3/4 cup (1 1/2 sticks) unsalted butter,
>   softened
> 1 1/2 cups peanut butter
> 1/2 cup sugar
> 3/4 cup firmly packed brown sugar
> 1 egg
> 1 teaspoon vanilla extract
> 1 1/2 cups all-purpose flour
> 1 teaspoon baking soda
> 1/4 teaspoon salt

■ Preheat the oven to 375°F. Lightly grease several cookie sheets.

■ Beat the butter and peanut butter together in a mixing bowl until creamy. Add the sugars gradually, beating until light. Beat in the egg and vanilla.

■ Mix the flour, baking soda, and salt and stir into the butter mixture, making a smooth dough.

■ Shape the dough into balls the size of a walnut and place them on cookie sheets about 1/2 inch apart. Press the dough balls flat with a fork.

■ Bake the cookies until firm and lightly browned, about 10 to 12 minutes.

Currant Pound Cake

MAKES one 9 x 5-inch loaf
PREPARATION: 30 minutes
COOKING: 60 minutes

A dense, buttery cake speckled with currants.

> 1 cup (2 sticks) unsalted buttter, softened
> 1 cup sugar
> 5 eggs
> 1/2 teaspoon vanilla extract
> 1/4 teaspoon freshly grated nutmeg
> 2 cups all-purpose flour
> 1 teaspoon baking powder
> 1/2 teaspoon salt
> 2 cups currants, dusted with 2
>   tablespoons flour

■ Preheat the oven to 325°F. Butter and flour a 9 x 5-inch loaf pan.

■ Beat the butter in a large mixing bowl until creamy. Add the sugar gradually, beating until smooth. Add the eggs 1 at a time, beating well after each addition. Stir in the vanilla and the nutmeg.

■ Combine the dry ingredients in a medium mixing bowl and mix well. Add the dry ingredients to the butter mixture and stir until no streaks of flour are visible. Fold in the currants and turn the batter into the prepared pan.

■ Bake in the oven until a toothpick inserted in the center comes out clean, about 60 minutes.

"Almost every person has something secret he likes to eat."

M. F. K. Fisher

Currant pound cake and strong coffee are always welcome on the night watch.

Honey date bars make teatime a satisfying afternoon break.

Honey Date Bars

MAKES 36 1 x 3-inch bars
PREPARATION: 20 minutes
COOKING: 25 minutes

These chewy and moist bars are also good in the evening with a small glass of port.

3 large eggs
1 cup honey, maple syrup, or Lyle's
  Golden Syrup
1 teaspoon vanilla extract
1½ cups all-purpose flour
½ teaspoon salt
½ teaspoon baking powder
1 pound pitted dates, coarsely chopped, or
  1 pound chopped dried apricots soaked
  in rum
1 cup coarsely chopped pecans
Confectioners' sugar, for coating

■ Preheat the oven to 350°F. Butter and flour a 9 x 13-inch baking pan, or line the pan with foil and butter the foil.

■ Beat the eggs in a large mixing bowl with the honey and vanilla until smooth. Mix the dry ingredients together in another large bowl and stir them into the egg mixture. Stir in the dates and pecans. Spread the batter in the pan.

■ Bake for 25 minutes, or until puffy and dry to the touch. Cool in the pan and cut into 1 x 3-inch bars. Dip the bars in confectioners' sugar and store in an airtight container. The bars will keep up to 3 weeks.

Note: Lyle's Golden Syrup is an English table syrup with a distinctive cane sugar flavor. Look for the ornate green and gold tin, found in any Caribbean supermarket or in gourmet food stores.

Apricot Oat Squares

MAKES 16 2-inch squares
PREPARATION: 15 minutes
COOKING: 20 minutes

Simple to prepare, this is the homey kind of dessert that everyone loves. Try substituting bitter marmalade or your favorite jam for the apricot preserves.

1 16-ounce jar apricot preserves
1 cup rolled oats
1 cup all-purpose flour
½ cup brown sugar
¼ teaspoon baking soda
8 tablespoons (1 stick) unsalted butter

■ Place the jar of preserves in hot water or a warm place until they are soft enough to spread.

■ Preheat the oven to 350°F. Butter an 8 x 8 x 2-inch baking pan.

■ Mix the dry ingredients in a large mixing bowl. Work the butter into the mixture with your fingertips until it resembles coarse crumbs. Press half of the mixture into the pan. Spread the warmed preserves over it evenly. Spread the remaining oat mixture on top, patting down lightly.

■ Bake until the top is lightly browned, about 20 minutes. Serve warm, spooned from the pan, with cream, yogurt, or ice cream. Or cool in the pan and cut into 2-inch squares.

Note: Use the oat mixture to make Banana Crisp (page 49).

"Cooking is like love. It should be entered into with abandon or not at all."

Harriet Van Horne

Midnight Suppers

As the sun sets on the Italian Riviera, the grand yachts pull into the jewel-like harbor of Portofino. Lounging on board are chic and sophisticated Europeans who return year after year to this romantic hideaway with its winding lanes, windswept trees, and tiny shops clustered around the harbor's edge.

Freshly showered, perpetually *abbronzatura*, and dressed in the inimitable European style known as throwaway chic, they hop into bright red inflatable dinghies and head for the alfresco bars, where they order tall Camparis and rummy cocktails. As the moon rises, twinkling lights and laughter fill the ancient seaside square.

Around eleven, couples stroll arm in arm down to the docks, where bobbing dinghies carry them back to sleek sailboats and power cruisers. On board, it's time for an intimate midnight supper *à deux*. The food is seductively simple: a pasta, perhaps, served with a good chilled champagne. At this hour, a light dish is enough to stave off hunger. Whether you're in Portofino, Italy, or Catalina, California, the following recipes are ideal for late, informal suppers or even a light lunch.

Pasta with Ham and Eggs

SERVES 2
PREPARATION: 20 minutes
COOKING: 10 minutes

This is Elizabeth's adaptation of a sternly correct recipe for *spaghetti ala carbonara*, which calls for an Italian cured bacon called pancetta. If you have pancetta, by all means use it. Otherwise, a flavorful ham works just as well.

½ pound thin spaghetti or linguine
2 tablespoons unsalted butter
2 or 3 slices pancetta, prosciutto, or country ham
2 to 3 garlic cloves, finely chopped
¼ to ½ teaspoon crushed red pepper
2 eggs
1 cup grated Parmesan cheese
Salt
Freshly ground pepper

■ Bring a large pot of salted water to a boil and begin cooking the pasta.

■ While the pasta cooks, heat the butter in a large skillet over low heat. Add the pancetta, garlic, and crushed pepper and sauté gently.

■ Beat the eggs lightly in a small mixing bowl with a handful of the cheese (about ¼ cup).

■ When the pasta is al dente, drain thoroughly and place it in the skillet. Working quickly, toss the pasta with the ham mixture and another handful of cheese. Add the eggs, tossing well, and salt and pepper to taste. Serve immediately with a dish of Parmesan for passing.

Variation: Fry the eggs until the whites are just set and the yolks are still runny, then slide them onto each portion of pasta so diners can break up the eggs and mix them into the pasta.

Thin Pasta with Chopped Fresh Tomato Sauce

SERVES 4
PREPARATION: 15 minutes
COOKING: 10 minutes

This is a dish for a hot night in deep summer, when tomatoes are lush and ripe. The taste of cold, juicy tomatoes with hot pasta is extraordinary.

6 large ripe tomatoes, peeled, seeded, and
* chopped (about 3 cups)*
2 garlic cloves, finely chopped
1 to 2 tablespoons white wine vinegar,
* Balsamic vinegar, or lemon juice*
4 to 5 tablespoons fruity olive oil
Fresh basil, parsley, or other fresh herb
Salt
Freshly ground pepper
1 pound thin spaghetti or angel hair
* pasta*

■ Place the tomatoes in a large bowl. Add the garlic, vinegar, oil, a few shredded basil leaves, and salt and pepper to taste. Stir.

■ Bring a large pot of salted water to a boil. Add the spaghetti and cook until al dente. Drain the spaghetti and dress it with a little olive oil.

■ Mound the pasta on plates and spoon the tomato sauce on top. Serve immediately with flasks of olive oil and vinegar at the table for seasoning.

Variation: Top the sauce with slivered black olives and crumbled feta cheese or mozzarella that has been marinating in oil. Or serve the sauce over couscous.

Angel Hair Pasta with Asparagus and Smoked Salmon

SERVES 2 to 3
PREPARATION: 10 minutes
COOKING: 20 minutes

The small vacuum-sealed packages of smoked salmon keep beautifully in the refrigerator, and are ideal for this special treat.

1½ cups heavy cream
½ pound thin fresh asparagus, trimmed
* and sliced at an angle into 1-inch*
* lengths*
½ pound dried angel hair pasta or thin
* spaghetti*
Salt
Freshly ground pepper
½ pound smoked salmon, cut into ribbons
* or squares*

■ Simmer the cream in a large skillet over medium heat until it thickens. Cover the pan and set the cream aside while preparing the remaining ingredients.

■ Fill a large saucepan with water and bring to a rolling boil. Add the asparagus and pasta and cook for about 5 minutes, until the asparagus is just tender and the pasta is al dente. (If using thin spaghetti, cook 2 or 3 minutes before adding the asparagus.)

■ Return the cream to the heat. Drain the pasta and asparagus immediately and turn them into the cream. Season the pasta lightly with salt and generously with pepper and fold in the smoked salmon. Serve immediately on warm plates.

Variation: Elizabeth made a variation of this for lunch on a blue-water passage, when she had no asparagus but did have a hunk of ripe St. André cheese and some smoked salmon. When the pasta was done, she tossed it with butter, salmon, globs of cheese, and plenty of freshly ground pepper. Everyone loved it.

TOMATO TIP
■

Although no one will stop you from leaving tomatoes unpeeled, once you experience the difference, the refinement is well worth the trouble.

Make peeling the tomatoes easier by dipping them in a saucepan of boiling water for a few seconds to loosen the skins, which will then slip off. Cut the tomatoes in half and scoop out the seeds with your finger or the handle of a spoon. Discard the skin and seeds.

Angel hair pasta with asparagus and smoked salmon can be made in short order to satisfy midnight appetites.

Eggs in hell.

Quesadilla

MAKES 1
PREPARATION: 10 minutes
COOKING: 10 minutes

A fast, south-of-the-border snack that is good by itself and even better with a spoonful of guacamole, a dollop of sour cream, and salsa.

2 large wheat tortillas
Monterey Jack, mild Cheddar, or
*   Muenster cheese, shredded*
Dried oregano
Scallions, finely sliced
Pickled jalapeño peppers, thinly sliced
Vegetable oil

■ Spread a tortilla flat on a plate. Spread a handful of cheese to within 1 inch of the edge. Sprinkle with a little oregano, a tablespoon or 2 of scallions, and a few slivers of jalapeños. Scatter a fine layer of cheese over all and cover with the other tortilla.

■ Heat a large skillet over medium heat. Swirl 2 or 3 teaspoons oil in the skillet until hot but not smoking. Slide the sandwich into the skillet and cook, adjusting the heat so the tortilla fries gently for about 2 minutes, or until the cheese begins to melt.

■ Flip the quesadilla carefully with a spatula and fry on the other side for 3 minutes until the cheese is melted and begins to ooze and sizzle in the pan. (If the idea of flipping a tortilla is daunting, invert a plate over the skillet and flip the quesadilla onto the plate, then slide it back into the skillet.)

■ Slide the finished quesadilla onto a cutting board and cut it into wedges with a sharp knife.

Note: To save dishwashing, assemble the quesadilla in the skillet. Put the tortilla in the hot skillet and, working quickly, add the ingredients as described above and cover with the second tortilla. Finish cooking the quesadilla as described.

Variation: Place 1 or 2 thin slices of tomato on the cheese and cover with a little more cheese before frying.

Comforting quesadillas are one of our favorite nocturnal snacks.

Migas

SERVES 2
PREPARATION: 10 minutes
COOKING: 10 minutes

These are Mexican-style eggs scrambled with peppers, tomatoes, and tortillas.

1 tablespoon vegetable oil
1 small green or red bell pepper, stems and seeds removed, thinly sliced
1 small onion, peeled and thinly sliced, or substitute 2 or 3 scallions, thinly sliced
1 ripe tomato, cored, seeded, and chopped, or about 3/4 cup drained canned tomatoes
4 to 5 large eggs
Salt
Freshly ground pepper
8 to 10 tortilla chips, roughly crushed

■ Heat the oil in a large skillet over medium heat. Add the pepper and onion and cook until softened. Add the tomato and cook, stirring, until most of the juice has evaporated.

■ Beat the eggs lightly and season to taste with salt and pepper. Pour the eggs into the skillet and cook, stirring, until they begin to solidify. Add the crushed tortilla chips and stir until the eggs are set. Serve immediately.

Variation: Add grated cheese, a spoonful of sour cream, or a few chunks of cream cheese to the eggs before pouring them into the pan. If you like, substitute canned green chiles for the fresh pepper.

Creamy Chicken Hash

SERVES 2 or 3
PREPARATION: 10 minutes
COOKING: 10 minutes

Hard-and-fast rules about hash do not exist. Add a diced cooked potato or a chopped pepper, or use scallions in place of the onion.

4 tablespoons (1/2 stick) unsalted butter
1 medium onion, finely chopped
1 tablespoon all-purpose flour
2 cups chopped cooked chicken
1/4 teaspoon dried thyme
2 tablespoons chopped fresh parsley
2 tablespoons sherry, Madeira, Cognac, or good port
3/4 cup heavy cream
Salt
Freshly ground pepper
Hot buttered toast, bread, or corn pancakes

Garnish
Sliced tomatoes

■ Heat the butter in a large skillet over medium heat. Add the onion and cook, stirring, until soft and translucent. Add the flour and cook for 2 minutes. Add the chicken, thyme, parsley, and sherry. Simmer for a few minutes, stirring gently. Add the cream and season to taste with salt and pepper. Allow the mixture to bubble gently until the cream thickens slightly. Taste for seasoning.

■ Spoon the hash onto hot toast, bread, or corn pancakes. Serve with sliced tomatoes.

Note: For a richer sauce, whisk the cream with an egg yolk before adding it to the simmering chicken, but be sure that the sauce does not curdle. Or, use Béchamel Sauce (page 145) or chicken gravy in lieu of the cream.

Goat Cheese Toasts

MAKES 4 large toasts
PREPARATION: 10 minutes
COOKING: 5 minutes

This savory snack is just enough to stay hunger after a long evening at play. Cut the bread at an angle to make large oval slices.

8 ¼-inch-thick slices Italian bread, cut
   at an angle
1 garlic clove, lightly crushed
Olive oil
1 ripe tomato, cored and thinly sliced
Salt
Freshly ground pepper
1 6½-ounce jar marinated artichoke
   hearts (optional)
2 5½-ounce packages goat cheese

■ Preheat the broiler (see Note).

■ Rub each bread slice with the garlic, brush them lightly with olive oil, and toast until lightly browned on both sides.

■ Place the slices on a baking pan. Cover each slice with tomato slices and season lightly with salt and pepper. Add a layer of sliced artichoke hearts. Place tablespoon-size pieces of the goat cheese on the artichokes and drizzle with olive oil. Return the toasts to the oven and broil until the cheese is lightly browned. Serve immediately.

Note: The toasts can also be prepared in a skillet. Prepare the bread as described above, then brown the toasts on both sides in a skillet over medium heat. Adjust the heat to low. Layer the ingredients on the toasts as described above and return them to the skillet. Cover the skillet and heat until the cheese softens.

Eggs in Hell

SERVES 4 to 6
PREPARATION: 15 minutes
COOKING: 20 minutes

Good for what ails you after a night of overindulgence.

2 tablespoons vegetable oil
1 small onion, chopped
1 garlic clove, chopped
1 or 2 3½-ounce cans green chiles,
   drained
2 teaspoons dried oregano
1 1-pound can crushed tomatoes in
   tomato puree
Salt
Tabasco
8 to 12 eggs

■ Heat the oil in a large, deep skillet over medium heat. Add the onion and garlic. Cook, stirring occasionally, until the vegetables are softened, about 10 minutes. Add the chiles, oregano, and tomatoes. Simmer the sauce until thickened. Season to taste with salt and a generous amount of Tabasco.

■ Lower the heat until the sauce barely bubbles and slip the eggs into the pan. Cover and cook the eggs until the whites are set.

■ Serve with corn tortillas, corn bread, fried potatoes, toast, or bread.

CREW DINNER
■
While cruising, the traditional way to thank your host is by picking up the tab for dinner ashore one night.

Offshore Racing

Several years ago during the Los Angeles-to-Honolulu TransPac race, a sailor smuggled fifty McDonald's Big Macs aboard his boat. Somehow he kept them hidden in the freezer until it was his turn to cook dinner. Then he popped the Styrofoam containers into the microwave and produced the famous hamburgers hundreds of miles offshore. The crew—adults who would hardly be tempted by the golden arches while driving along America's highways—went wild.

This clever fellow understood an important aspect of ocean racing: Food is of primary importance. This is especially true on long passages, where thrilling hours on a thundering spinnaker reach can be supplanted by terrifying nights in a vicious gale or boring days becalmed on a vast ocean. Seasoned sailors will agree that food is the best way to ease the strain and considerable discomforts—wet clothes, sporadic sleep, hot bunking, and the constant pressure to win—of offshore racing.

One way to boost the sagging spirits of exhausted sailors is to serve food associated with the shore. Even if you can't

procure Big Macs, a cake brought on board in anticipation of someone's birthday or French toast served with real maple syrup will work wonders.

Another way is to make food look as appealing as possible. It doesn't matter if a garnish is part of a recipe or a perfect complement to the food, as long as it looks good. A drab beef stew can be dressed up (in calm seas, of course) with a few slivers of red pepper, a scattering of parsley leaves, some shredded scallions or carrots, pickled red onions, or orange slices.

Racing is dramatically different from cruising, and demanding for the cook as well as the crew. Conditions are rougher, restocking is impossible, and meals must be served at a prescribed time. You can make things a good deal easier for yourself by doing *every possible preparation* ashore. The one-dish meals that follow can be made at home and frozen, then taken aboard. Hearty and nutritious, these casseroles are ideal for racing, and also for long cruises.

". . . our black cook; who according to the invariable custom at sea, always went by the name of the doctor.

And doctors, cooks certainly are; the very best medicos in the world . . ."

Herman Melville,
Redburn

Freezing and Reheating Instructions

Stews and casseroles can be frozen successfully. Vegetables in dishes to be frozen should be slightly undercooked since they will finish cooking while the dish is heated. Since potatoes do not freeze well, it is best to cook them while the dish is reheating and add them.

To freeze casseroles: Before freezing the casserole, adjust the freezer temperature to the lowest setting.

Whether the casserole is assembled or poured into a disposable aluminum baking pan, the cook should allow head space of about 1½ inches to avoid leaking and to allow for expansion. When cool, place a sheet of aluminum foil flat on the surface of the food to exclude air. Then affix a flat aluminum lid, crimping the edges under carefully. Place the casserole in the freezer without crowding, preferably on the floor of the freezer, directly over the freezer plates or coils. Freeze for about 12 hours or until solid. Label the casserole and include heating and serving instructions on a slip of paper if desired. Double wrap in plastic bags for storage.

To reheat casseroles: For best results casseroles should be thawed first before heating. Thaw in the refrigerator or an icebox for about 8 hours until a knife inserted in the center can go through to the bottom of the casserole. Heat the casserole as directed in each recipe.

People living on boats pay particular attention to the conservation of electric and fuel energy and water. It makes sense to use the cooling energy of a frozen casserole in a cooler, to reduce the energy demands of a refrigerator, or to extend the life of ice in an icebox. This practice also saves the extra fuel energy needed to heat a solidly frozen casserole.

Pastitsio

SERVES 8
PREPARATION: 60 minutes
COOKING: 40 minutes

This is a hearty dish of Greek origin made of meat and macaroni and covered with a creamy custard.

1 pound elbow macaroni
¼ cup oil
1 large onion, chopped
1 celery stalk with leaves, chopped
2 pounds lean ground beef
1 teaspoon dried oregano
1 teaspoon crushed red pepper
1 28-ounce can crushed tomatoes
2 cups freshly grated Parmesan or Asiago cheese
Salt
Freshly ground pepper
3 cups Béchamel Sauce (recipe follows)
3 eggs
1 pound (2 cups) ricotta cheese

■ Preheat the oven to 350°F.

■ Bring a large pot of salted water to a boil. Cook the macaroni in the water until slightly undercooked. Drain the macaroni, cool under cold running water, and drain again.

■ Heat the oil in a large skillet over medium heat. Add the onion and the celery. Cook, stirring, until the vegetables have softened. Add the beef, oregano, and pepper flakes and cook, stirring to break up the meat, until the beef loses its pink color. Pour off the excess fat. Add the tomatoes and cook, stirring occasionally, about 30 minutes.

■ Lightly oil 2 12 x 8 x 2-inch aluminum pans. Divide half the macaroni between the 2 pans and spread it into even layers. Sprinkle each layer with 2 tablespoons Parmesan cheese and salt and pepper to taste. Spread the meat mixture on top and cover with the remaining macaroni. Sprinkle each layer with 2 tablespoons more Parmesan cheese and additional salt and pepper.

■ Make the Béchamel Sauce and allow it to cool slightly. Whisk the eggs into the sauce, beating well to prevent the eggs from curdling. Add the ricotta and all but 4 tablespoons of the Parmesan. Stir until smooth, then pour the sauce over the macaroni. Sprinkle the remaining Parmesan over the top of teach pan.

■ Bake the casseroles until bubbling and set, about 40 minutes. See freezing instructions on page 144.

Variation: Although tasty when made with freshly ground meat, this dish is also delicious with leftover roast beef, pork, or lamb. Substitute 4 cups of any of these for the ground beef.

Suggested Wine: A dry light red such as Chianti.

Béchamel Sauce

MAKES 3½ cups
PREPARATION: 30 minutes

6 tablespoons (¾ stick) unsalted butter
6 tablespoons all-purpose flour
3 cups milk
Salt
Freshly ground pepper
Freshly grated nutmeg
Tabasco

■ Melt the butter in a saucepan over medium heat. Add the flour and cook, stirring, about 5 minutes.

■ Meanwhile, bring the milk to a boil over medium heat. Add the milk to the butter and flour mixture all at once and stir vigorously with a whisk until smooth. Cook the sauce over low heat, stirring frequently, for 20 minutes. Season with salt, pepper, nutmeg, and Tabasco. Cover until ready to use.

RACING TIPS
■

· Serve fresh salad often. Iceberg lettuce keeps well, as does Romaine lettuce, radicchio, cabbage, and endive.

· Store chocolate bars and soft candy in a plastic bag in the ice box.

· Keep a designated snack locker stocked with quick energizers such as cheese, crackers, cookies, nuts, dried fruits, granola bars, apples, oranges, small boxes of raisins, and bags of trail mix.

· Allow for larger appetites than on land.

· Don't forget the Champagne for the victory celebration!

Liz passes lunch topside.

Close action at the windward mark.

New York Yacht Club Race Committee in the midst of a starting sequence.

Jockeying for position at the start of the race.

Curried Turkey

SERVES 8 to 10 generously
PREPARATION: 30 minutes
COOKING: 45 minutes

Although not authentically Indian, this curried dish charms most people, particularly Aussies and others of British extraction. It's also quite easy to eat—no small comfort on a raging sea.

5 pounds uncooked boneless skinless turkey breast, cut into 1-inch pieces
4 to 5 tablespoons good curry powder
3 tablespoons finely chopped or grated fresh ginger root
¼ cup cider vinegar or white wine vinegar
2 teaspoons hot red pepper flakes
8 tablespoons (1 stick) unsalted butter
2 large onions, chopped
3 to 4 garlic cloves, chopped (optional)
5 celery stalks, cut in ¼-inch pieces
2 bay leaves
¾ cup all-purpose flour
3 quarts chicken broth, heated
4 tart apples, such as Granny Smith, peeled, cored, and cut into ½-inch pieces

■ Put the turkey in a large mixing bowl with the curry, ginger, vinegar, and pepper flakes. Rub the spices into the turkey pieces and set aside.

■ Heat the butter in a large, heavy pot over medium heat. Add the onions, garlic, celery, and bay leaves and cook, stirring, until the vegetables are softened, about 10 minutes. Add the flour and cook, stirring, for about 5 minutes. Add the spiced turkey and turn it in the pot continually until it begins to whiten and the spices are aromatic. Add the chicken broth gradually, stirring well. Add the apples. Simmer the curry gently about 45 minutes, stirring so that the sauce doesn't scorch. Taste for seasoning (remembering that freezing will mute the flavors).

■ Cool the curry and pour into foil containers. See freezing instructions on page 144.

■ Serve with plenty of rice and condiments such as roasted peanuts, cashews, almonds, or macadamia nuts; a good chutney; dried shredded coconut; dried raisins, apricots, figs, or currants; canned pineapple chunks; chopped raw onion; plain yogurt, etc.

Chicken Cobbler

SERVES 10
PREPARATION: 60 minutes
COOKING: 90 minutes

This mild down-home cobbler is comforting in rough weather.

2 3-pound chickens
2 cups dry white wine
2 celery stalks, sliced
2 sprigs fresh parsley
1 bay leaf
2 whole cloves
6 carrots, cut into ½-inch slices
8 tablespoons (1 stick) unsalted butter
2 large onions, chopped
½ cup all-purpose flour
2 cups milk
1 tablespoon dried tarragon
¼ cup chopped fresh parsley
2 to 3 teaspoons salt
Freshly ground pepper
¼ teaspoon freshly grated nutmeg

Cobbler Dough
2 cups all-purpose flour
½ teaspoon salt
1 teaspoon baking powder
8 tablespoons (1 stick) unsalted butter, softened
4 to 5 tablespoons cold milk

■ Put the chickens in a large pot. Add the wine and sufficient cold water to cover. Add the celery, parsley sprigs, bay leaf, and cloves. Bring the water to a boil, then reduce the heat and simmer until the chicken is tender, about 40 minutes. Remove the chicken, cool, and remove all skin and bones. Pull the meat into large chunks. Strain the broth and reserve 2 cups.

- Steam the carrots until slightly crunchy and set aside to cool.

- Melt the butter in a large, heavy saucepan over medium heat. Add the onions and cook until softened. Add the flour and cook, stirring, about 5 minutes. Gradually add the reserved broth, stirring constantly with a whisk until the sauce is thickened and smooth. Whisk in the milk and add the tarragon and chopped parsley and salt, pepper, and nutmeg to taste. Stir in the reserved chicken pieces and the carrots. Taste, and correct seasonings.

- Pour the chicken filling into a 9 x 12 x 2-inch foil container with a foil lid. Leave about ½ inch headroom. Allow the filling to cool, then freeze it.

- To make the cobbler dough place the flour, salt, and baking powder in a large mixing bowl. Work the butter into the flour until the mixture resembles coarse meal. Stir in the milk and mix until the dough clings together. Pat the dough into a disk and refrigerate until ready to use.

- Roll out the dough about ¼-inch thick on a floured surface. Drape the dough over the chicken filling, tucking the edges under along the sides. (Or cut the dough into circles, squares, or triangles and place overlapping pieces on top of the chicken filling.)

- Preheat the oven to 350°F.

- Defrost and then bake the cobbler, uncovered, until the crust is brown, about 40 minutes.

Variation: Add other vegetables such as corn, peas, blanched green beans, zucchini, or peppers to this dish.

Suggested Wine: A dry white, such as Sauvignon Blanc or Semillon.

Meat Loaf

MAKES 2 large loaves
PREPARATION: 30 minutes
COOKING: 60 minutes

If you intend to freeze this dish, undercook it slightly. When finished on board, the meat loaf will be juicy.

2½ pounds ground beef chuck
1½ pounds ground pork
3 tablespoons vegetable oil
2 medium onions, finely chopped
2 garlic cloves, finely chopped (optional)
1 cup chopped fresh parsley
3 to 4 teaspoons salt
2 teaspoons freshly ground pepper
1 teaspoon ground allspice (optional)
2 teaspoons sweet Hungarian paprika (optional)
2 teaspoons dried marjoram
2 cups fresh bread crumbs, or 1½ cups uncooked rolled oats
1 cup tomato juice
3 eggs, beaten

- Preheat the oven to 350°F.

- In a large mixing bowl, break the meat apart with a fork.

- Heat the oil in a skillet over medium heat. Add the onion and garlic and cook, partially covered, until the onion is translucent, about 5 minutes. Cool the onions and scrape them into the meat mixture. Add the remaining ingredients and mix well with your hands.

- Oil 2 12 x 8 x 2-inch pans. Divide the meat mixture between the pans and flatten into loaves. Set the pans on a baking pan to catch any bubbling juices.

- Bake in the oven about 1 hour. Remove the loaves from the oven while the juices still run pink. Allow the loaves to cool completely before freezing. See freezing instructions on page 144.

Variation: Divide 2 cups tomato sauce between the pans and spoon it over the meat loaf while it cooks.

Suggested Wine: Zinfandel.

See freezing instructions on page 144.

HEAVY-WEATHER HINTS
■

· Allow more time than usual to prepare a meal.

· Use heavy pans with heavy, tight-fitting lids.

· Serve soup, cereal, and one-dish meals in mugs or deep bowls.

· Use clamp arms to keep pots in place over the stove burners.

· Don't be insulted if the crew isn't hungry—you may not be the only one with a queasy stomach!

Beef Stew with Red Wine

SERVES 12 to 14
PREPARATION: 45 minutes
COOKING: 2½ hours

Hearty and soul satisfying on a cold rainy night.

8 pounds beef rump or chuck, cut into 2-inch pieces
Salt
Freshly ground pepper
1 cup vegetable oil
8 large onions, chopped
12 carrots, cut into ¼-inch slices
1 cup all-purpose flour
1 tablespoon dried thyme
1 tablespoon dried marjoram
2 bay leaves
6 cups dry red or white wine
2 cups ripe tomatoes, peeled, seeded, and chopped
¼ cup Dijon mustard
3 pounds cultivated mushrooms

Vegetable oil
Unsalted butter
1 cup chopped fresh parsley
Grated rind of 1 lemon

■ Pat the beef dry and place it in a mixing bowl. Rub the beef with salt and a generous amount of pepper.

■ Heat the oil in a large, wide, heavy pot. Brown the meat in small batches and set aside as the pieces are done. Season with additional salt.

■ Add the vegetables to the pan and cook until softened, about 10 minutes. Add the flour and cook, stirring, about 10 minutes. Stir in the herbs, then the meat. Add the wine gradually, stirring constantly. Add the tomatoes and mustard. If necessary, add water to cover the meat. Simmer the stew until the meat is tender, about 2½ hours. Skim the fat and foam from the surface of the liquid.

■ Cook the mushrooms in batches in a large skillet with a mixture of oil and butter. Season with salt and pepper and, when mushrooms are tender, add the parsley and lemon rind. Stir the mushrooms into the stew.

■ Cool the beef stew and spoon into foil containers. See freezing instructions on page 144.

Chicken Chili

SERVES 8
PREPARATION: 30 minutes
COOKING: 45 minutes

½ cup vegetable oil
4 pounds boneless skinless chicken or turkey, cut into 1-inch pieces
2 medium onions, chopped
4 garlic cloves, chopped (optional)
4 red bell peppers, stemmed, seeded, and sliced
4 fresh jalapeño peppers, stemmed, seeded, and sliced
6 tablespoons chili powder
2 tablespoons ground cumin
1 tablespoon dried oregano
⅛ teaspoon cinnamon
2 28-ounce cans crushed tomatoes in puree
1 12-ounce can beer or 1½ cups chicken broth
Salt

■ Heat the oil in a large skillet over medium-high heat. Sauté the chicken or turkey in batches until lightly browned on all sides, setting the pieces aside as they are cooked.

■ Lower the heat and add the onions, garlic, and peppers to the skillet. Cook, stirring, until the vegetables are softened. Add the chili powder, cumin, oregano, and cinnamon and simmer for 2 or 3 minutes. Add the tomatoes and beer and simmer until the sauce is thickened, about 20 minutes. Salt to taste.

■ Return the chicken to the skillet and simmer until the chicken is done, about 20 minutes. Test seasoning and serve with the condiments.

■ Cool the chili and spoon into foil containers. See freezing instructions on page 144.

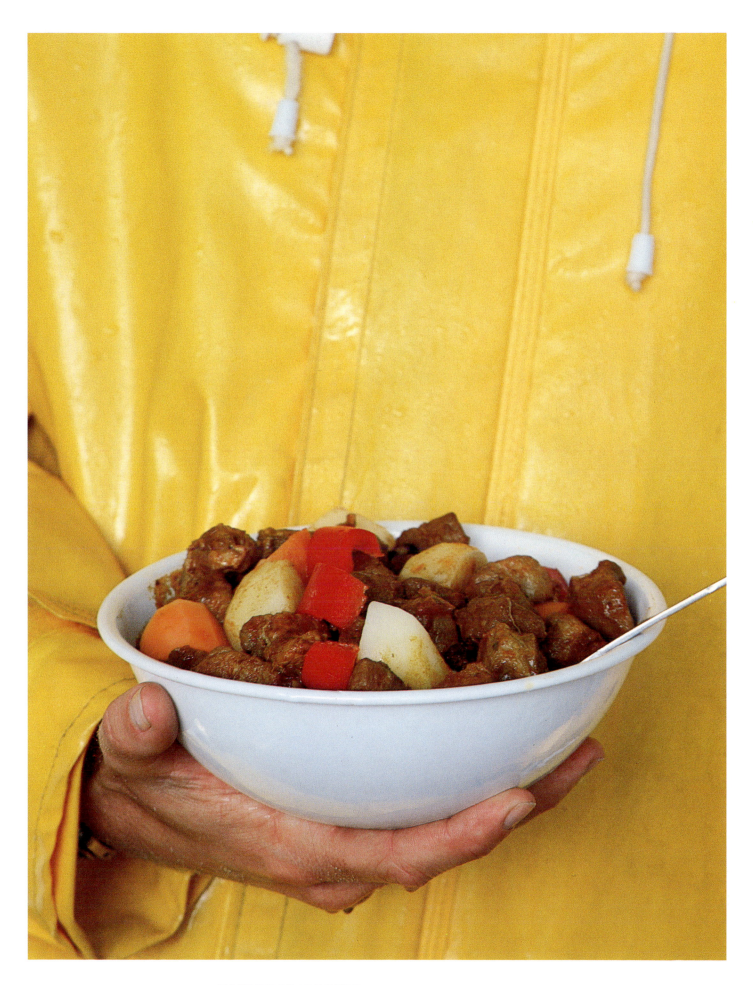

Three-Cheese Lasagna with Meat Sauce

SERVES 12
PREPARATION: 30 minutes
COOKING: about 1½ hours for the sauce plus 45 minutes for baking

This lasagna belongs on a boat full of hungry people who have been exerting themselves.

Sauce
½ cup olive oil or vegetable oil
2 large onions (about 1 pound), peeled and chopped
2 to 3 garlic cloves, peeled and chopped (optional)
2 celery stalks, chopped
2 large carrots, peeled and chopped
2 pounds lean ground beef
1 pound sweet or hot Italian sausage, casings removed
3 28-ounce cans whole tomatoes
2 tablespoons dried oregano
2 tablespoons dried basil
¼ teaspoon ground cloves
Freshly ground pepper
Salt

Filling
2 pounds ricotta cheese
¼ cup finely chopped fresh parsley
2 pounds mozzarella cheese, cut into ¼-inch cubes
2 cups freshly grated Parmesan or Asiago cheese
4 eggs, lightly beaten
Salt
Freshly ground pepper

24 lasagna noodles
Béchamel Sauce (page 145)

■ To make the tomato sauce, heat the oil in a large pot over medium heat. Add the onions, garlic, celery, and carrots. Cook, stirring, until the vegetables have softened slightly, about 5 minutes. Add the beef and sausage and cook, stirring to break up the meat, until it loses its pink color. Pour off the excess fat. Add the tomatoes, crushing them through your fingers, and the herbs, spices, and salt. Simmer the sauce about 1½ hours, stirring occasionally, or until thick.

■ To make the filling, mix the ricotta, parsley, mozzarella, 1½ cups Parmesan, and the eggs in a large mixing bowl. Stir well to combine, and add salt and pepper to taste.

■ Bring a large pot of salted water to a boil. Cook the noodles 6 or 8 at a time, and when they are almost tender but still firm, transfer them to a large bowl filled with cold water. Lift the noodles from the cold water, gently strip off the water with your fingers, and spread them on a cloth in a single layer. (Cooking the noodles is much easier if a large, deep-frying type wire basket is first set in the boiling water. This way, when the noodles are cooked, they can be lifted from the water all at once.)

■ Preheat the oven to 350°F.

■ To assemble the lasagna, lightly oil 3 12 x 8 x 2-inch aluminum pans. Spread a thin layer of meat sauce on the bottom of each pan. Cover with a layer of noodles. Spread a ½-inch layer of the cheese filling onto the noodles. Spread a layer of meat sauce over the filling. Cover with another layer of noodles, and continue layering, ending with the noodles. Spread a layer of the Béchamel Sauce over the noodles. Carefully run a knife along the sides of the pan to allow the sauce to settle into the casserole. Sprinkle the top with the remaining Parmesan.

■ Bake the lasagna about 45 minutes, or until bubbling and lightly browned on top. Cool completely before wrapping and freezing. See freezing instructions on page 144.

Suggested wine: Zinfandel, Barbaresco, or Montepulciano.

Shepherd's Pie

SERVES 4 to 6
PREPARATION: 30 minutes
COOKING: 2 hours

This is a sturdy, straightforward dish that sailors love. Nothing fancy, but it is met with enthusiasm every time.

2 tablespoons vegetable oil
2 pounds lean ground beef or lamb, or 4
     to 5 cups chopped cooked beef or lamb
4 medium onions, thinly sliced
Salt
Freshly ground pepper
¼ cup all-purpose flour
1 10-ounce can beef broth
2 12-ounce cans beer
2 bay leaves
1 tablespoon brown sugar
2 to 3 tablespoons Worcestershire sauce
6 carrots, peeled and cut into 1-inch
     lengths
1 to 2 tablespoons prepared horseradish
1 10-ounce package frozen peas, defrosted
2 pounds small red boiling potatoes,
     peeled and quartered
2 tablespoons melted unsalted butter
½ cup milk (approximately)
Freshly grated nutmeg
Butter

■ Heat the oil in a large skillet over medium-high heat. Add the meat and cook, stirring, until browned. Lower the heat, add the onions, and cook until softened. Season to taste with salt and pepper. Add the flour and cook 3 minutes. Gradually add the broth, beer, bay leaves, sugar, and Worcestershire sauce. Bring the liquid to a boil, lower the heat, and cook, partially covered, for 1 hour, skimming any excess fat. Add the carrots and continue to cook until they are tender. Remove the bay leaves and stir in the horseradish and peas. Divide the mixture between 2 12 x 8 x 2-inch aluminum pans and freeze, if desired.

■ To serve, preheat the oven to 375°F. Defrost casserole if frozen. Steam or boil the potatoes until tender. Drain, retaining a little cooking liquid in the pot, and mash with a fork. Stir in the butter and enough milk to make a smooth puree. Season to taste with salt, pepper, and nutmeg and spread over the meat. Add a few shavings of butter to the tops.

■ Bake the pie until it is bubbling and lightly browned, about 20 minutes.

Variation: Slice the raw potatoes ⅛-inch thick and place in overlapping slices on top of the meat mixture, covering it completely. Brush the potatoes lightly with melted butter and season to taste with salt and pepper. (Do not freeze this dish once the potatoes have been cooked.)

Suggested Wine: Zinfandel.

"Interviewer: Could you please tell us, in your own words, why did the Intrepid *lose the race?*

Cook: Well, I suppose it was my fault. I started preparing the Bouillabaise as we rounded the last buoy. We were way ahead, and when the soup was ready I called the crew down to the galley. I really don't know what happened after that, except that when we went back up on deck we were sailing in somebody's wake. But on one point everyone's agreed. That was the most fantastic Bouillabaise I've ever made."

Neil Hollander and
Harald Mertes

Getting Ready

Once, in the interest of economy, Jennifer bought a ten-pound wheel of Cheddar cheese for a thousand-mile sailing trip. She didn't think it so economical when, four days later, she was forced to throw most of the waterlogged wheel (the entire cheese supply) overboard. Another time Elizabeth bought 16 cases of dark Heineken beer for a month-long passage, only to learn—too late—that everyone preferred light beer.

Our crews were forgiving, and we learned from our mistakes. Dozens of cruises later—our notebooks filled with menus served on trips to Maine, Mustique, and New Guinea—we now realize that, with a little organization, planning, and boat sense, provisioning needn't be a nightmare. Here are some guidelines we've learned along the way.

Menus: Before setting foot on a boat, plan a framework of menus for the entire trip to guarantee that you buy enough food for all the meals. Of course, this doesn't mean that when you're in Antigua on Wednesday you have to eat lemon chicken because you planned it five weeks ago at home. Rather, plan flexibly to allow for situations that come up (weather, occasions, etc.), while still ensuring that everyone will be well fed.

When preparing a shopping list, remember that people eat and drink more on the water than on land. Query your crew on food preferences, then make a detailed list of the items you will need and the quantity of each. With eggs, for example, calculate the number needed for breakfast, lunch, and baking, plus a few extras to allow for loss and breakage. If you're planning a long trip, bear in mind that at sea, especially when isolated on a vast ocean, people like more sweets and junk food than they ever would admit to on land.

When purchasing beverages, consider two factors: thirst (from exposure) and boredom. When Elizabeth provisioned for a cruise from Honolulu to Papua New Guinea, she calculated one cup of juice (at least) and five servings of soda, seltzer, or beer per person per day in addition to the beverages served with meals. When buying milk, remember that it will be used for cooking, cereals, and coffee. Stock up, too, on evaporated milk and Longlife, which work well for coffee and cooking when the fresh milk supply runs out.

Shopping: It may sound obvious but bears mentioning: Buy the least perishable items first. Up to a week before departure, buy canned goods and packaged items (in sizes you'll be likely to consume quickly rather than economy sizes) and stow them on the boat. The day before departure, chill the refrigerator before buying the perishables. Always unpack paper bags and cardboard boxes on the dock and hand items over to someone in the cockpit; otherwise, you're inviting the local insect population aboard. (If you're planning a long passage, strip cans of their labels, which also harbor insects

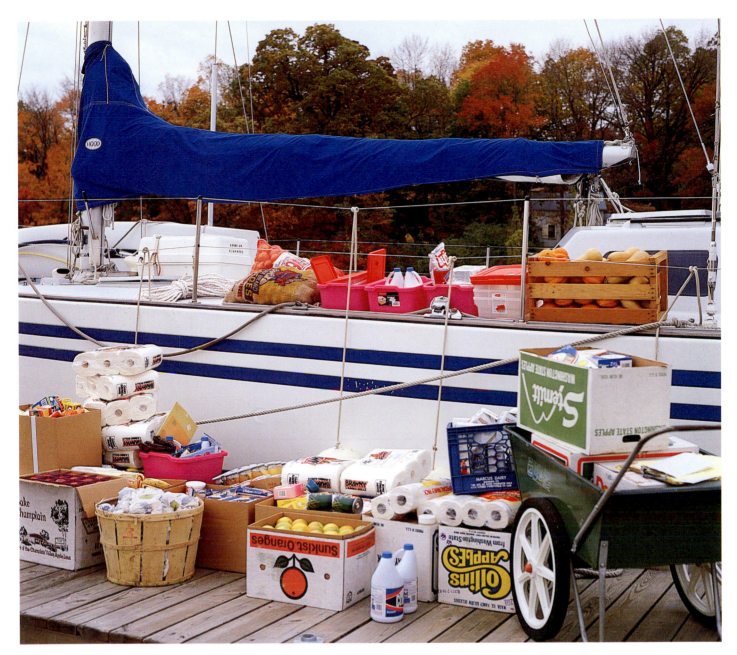

and eggs, while you're still at the dock, then mark cans with an indelible pen.)

Packaging: Blot dry fresh produce with toweling and remove any dead leaves, stems, etc. before stowing in the refrigerator. (Don't wash produce, however, until you're preparing the meal, as moisture hastens rot.) Store the produce in plastic bags or sturdy plastic boxes. We put all the steaks in one Tupperware box, for example, to prevent them from dripping or getting dripped on. Sticks of butter are also best kept in a plastic box. The more you compartmentalize, the easier finding items under way will be. You'll also cut down on contamination and bruising, lengthening the life of fresh food.

To save time and aggravation at sea, mix the dry ingredients for pancakes, muffins, cookies, etc. ahead of time, and store them in plastic containers along with the recipe written on a slip of paper.

Organization: We can't emphasize enough how crucial organization is on a boat. The cook should be in charge of devising some system of stowing food and supplies. We usually pack items according to products (canned vegetables in locker A, dry goods in locker B, etc.), while others swear by packing lockers according to menus. Record on a master

Some tips to get the most out of your refrigeration:

· On short trips, chill soft drinks and beer before taking them aboard.

· Freeze water and juice in plastic jugs before taking them aboard.

· If you're using a cooler, don't drain the ice water, as it keeps the rest of the ice from melting too rapidly.

· If the refrigerator is full, chill wine by dangling it overboard in a net.

list what is in each locker, then check off each item as it is consumed.

Stowage: Pack the refrigerator in a logical fashion, with heavy perishables such as frozen meat stored closest to the ice or refrigeration plate and delicate items packed near the surface. Store frozen foods together and they'll stay frozen longer.

On long passages, especially, keep a separate drinks cooler readily available. You don't want someone diving to the bottom of the refrigerator—upsetting everything—because he's convinced there's one more Molson down there. You can transfer the next day's supply of drinks from the bilge to the refrigerator every evening; then, in the mornings, move the chilled drinks to the cooler on deck.

The first few nights: On any cruise people (cook often included) take a few days to get their sea legs. To compensate, we often precook a few dinners, hors d'oeuvres, and cookies before leaving the dock. It makes the first few days at sea much more pleasant.

Snacks: To avoid conflicts but allow the crew freedom to get their own snacks, designate a snack locker that can be accessed at any time. And remember to keep it well stocked! We learned this the hard way several years ago on a passage from North Carolina to Virgin Gorda when the ravenous first mate disappeared into the galley to make a snack. He appeared on deck an hour later with a glorious pizza heaped with sausage, anchovies, peppers, and cheese. It was absolutely delicious . . . but it also contained most of the food intended for the next two lunches.

A word about plastics: On boats, plastic bags and sturdy plastic boxes are invaluable. We pack almost all of our food in plastics, and even such dry items as cereals, rice, crackers, and packaged mixes go in plastic bags inside airtight plastic containers. The combination keeps food clean, dry, and contained, and—most important—does wonders for preserving the sea cook's sanity.

Unrefrigerated produce: Many fresh fruits, cheeses, and vegetables can be kept unrefrigerated for weeks on boats. Some tips we've learned over the years:

Hard fruits and vegetables (potatoes, onions, apples, etc.) can be stored for more than three weeks in secured hanging nets in dark, cool, well-ventilated places.

Soft-skinned fruits and vegetables (pears, oranges, cucumbers, etc.) can be bought while hard (and papayas, bananas, mangoes, and tomatoes while still green). Wrap produce individually in tissue or newspaper and store in single layers (to prevent rotting), snugly packed (to prevent rolling and bruising). Pears stored this way will last two weeks, whereas oranges can last a month.

Citrus fruit can be dipped in a solution of one gallon of water and one cup of chlorine bleach (to slow rot and fungus) and dried in the sun before wrapping in paper and packing snugly.

Cabbages can be bought hard, with the outer leaves intact, and stored in nets for up to three weeks.

Eggs will stay fresh 4 to 5 weeks if coated with petroleum jelly or solid shortening and kept in a cool place. If possible, buy farm-fresh eggs that have never been refrigerated.

Well-aged hard cheeses (Parmesan, provolone, Romano) keep longer than soft young cheeses. Wrap cut cheeses tightly in cheesecloth moistened with vinegar and store in a cool, dark place. For longer storage, wrap one-pound pieces of cheese as described above and dip in melted paraffin several times, allowing each coat to harden before dipping again.

Canned Brie and Camembert are convenient luxuries to have on board, and some types can be stored unrefrigerated for a short time.

Check fruit and vegetables daily, and adjust the menu schedule accordingly as produce ripens.

Tools of the Trade

While you don't need elaborate equipment to produce wonderful food, certain items are helpful in a galley. We recommend:

Pots and Pans
2 stainless-steel saucepans (1½- and 2-quart), with lids
Large kettle or pot (large enough to hold lobsters, clams, etc.), with lid and perforated insert (which can double as a colander)
2 heavy skillets (8- and 12-inch), with lids
Pressure cooker (4- to 8-quart), with steamer insert
Roasting pans
Casserole dishes

Miscellaneous Essentials
Water kettle
Coffee percolator
Nested mixing bowls (plastic or stainless-steel)
Sturdy Tupperware containers of various sizes, with lids
Pie plates, baking pans, cookie sheets
Measuring cups and spoons
Wood or plastic cutting boards (A small one with a handle is the most useful.)

Tools
2 paring knives (because they often disappear)
Serrated knife
All-purpose chopping knife
Wire sieve
Wire whisk
Pastry brush
Wooden mixing spoons
Slotted spoon
All-purpose poultry shears
Can and bottle opener
Corkscrew
Stainless-steel box grater
Vegetable peelers (several)
Rubber spatula
Ice pick

Serving Implements
Metal spatula
Stainless-steel tongs (We prefer the pincer type with scalloped teeth.)
Ladle
Large forks
Large spoons
Plastic pitcher

THE FRUIT AND THE NUTS

■

For Trail Mix Deluxe, mix any or all of these: 1 pound whole almonds, 1 pound walnut halves, 1 pound pecan halves, 1 pound cashew nuts, 1 pound dried sliced bananas, 1 pound toasted coconut chips, 1 pound Monukka raisins, 2 pounds dried apricots, 2 pounds M&Ms chocolate candies, and 1 pound sesame candies. Store in airtight containers and keep handy for snacking.

Index

smoked chicken salad with pecans and, 129

dips:
  parslied chick-pea, 101
  quick, 93
  smoky eggplant, 13
dumplings, one-pot Hungarian chicken with, 44, 45

Eggplant:
  dip, smoky, 13
  grilled, 13   *deviledeggs97*
  salad, Italian, 88
eggs:
  hard-boiled, 77
  in Hell, 141
  Mexican-style scrambled, 140
  pasta with ham and, 136
  scrambled, under-way, 119
  storage of, 156

Fish:
  barbecued, with potatoes and vegetables, 29
  chowder, Ernestina's, 52–53
  filleting of, 88
  grilling of, 29
  killing of, 88
  marinated raw (poisson crû), 100
  old-fashioned pickled, 89
  panfried trout with bacon, 61
  poisonous, 104
  smoked salmon, angel hair pasta with asparagus and, 137
  see also bluefish
French toast, 120
fried apples, 122
frittata, pepper, ham, and potato, 68
fritters, cornmeal, 64
fruit:
  and nuts, 150
  salad, 69
  storage of, 156
  see also specific fruits

Garlic:
  bread, 49
  vinaigrette, 77
gas grills, 16
gazpacho, grated, 28
gingerbread men, 108
ginger chicken, grilled, 24
granola, 116
gratin of sweet and white potatoes, 36–37
gravlax with mustard sauce, 100
green bean and tomato salad, 25
greens, 32, 40
green salad, 32
green sauce, 97
grilled dishes, 12–16, 22–27
  bluefish with Aquavit, 89
  bluefish with tomatoes and onions, 89
  breakfast sandwich, 122
  butterflied lamb with mustard vinaigrette, 20
  cabbage, 14
  eggplant, 13
  filet of beef with mushroom sauce, 33
  ginger chicken, 24
  grill-roasted fish with potatoes and vegetables, 29

kinds of grills for, 16
lime-marinated pork, 12–13
marinated tuna, 28–29
pineapple, 16
pumpkin, 14
skewered chicken with green sauce, 97
smoky flavor in, 20
spicy skewered beef with peanut sauce, 96
tips for, 13
tips on fish as, 29
see also roasted dishes
guacamole, 57

Ham:
  pasta with eggs and, 136
  pepper, and potato frittata, 68
hard sauce, 45
hash, creamy chicken, 140
heavy-weather, cooking tips for, 149
honey date bars, 135
hors d'oeuvres, 92–95
Hungarian chicken with dumplings, one-pot, 44–45

Italian bread, tomato and mozzarella sandwiches on, 76–77
Italian eggplant salad, 88

Jambalaya, chicken, 48

Knives, sharp, 136

Lamb:
  grilled butterflied, with mustard vinaigrette, 20
  in shepherd's pie, 153
lasagna, three-cheese, with meat sauce, 152
lemons:
  bars, 132
  chicken wings, 84
  sautéed bluefish with capers and, 89
limes:
  Caribbean lobsters with, 104
  -marinated pork, grilled, 12–13
  pie, 26
  syrup, 27
linguiça with peppers, 53
liquado, banana, 27
lobster:
  Caribbean, with limes, 104
  Creole, 105

Macaroni and beef (pastitsio), 145
marinated dishes:
  chick-pea salad, 129
  herbed cheese, 94
  pork, grilled lime-, 12–13
  raw fish (poisson crû), 100
  steak salad, 123
  tuna, grilled, 28–29
  zucchini salad, 124
mayonnaise, 104
meat, see specific meats
meatloaf, 149
melon, fresh, 32
menus, framework of, 154
Mexican banana liquado, 27
Mexican-style scrambled eggs (migas), 140
migas, 140
minestrone, hearty, 48

muffins:
  buttermilk bran, 117
  spiced apple, 117
mushroom sauce, 33, 36
mussels with herbs, 38
mustard:
  butter, 93
  sauce, 100
  vinaigrette, 20

Nautical nuggets, 111
nuts:
  fruit and, 150
  see also specific nuts

Oat, apricot squares, 135
oatmeal, 117
olives, tomato salad with feta cheese and, 17
onions:
  beef stew with beer and, 44
  grilled bluefish with tomatoes and, 89
  pickled, and beet salad, 128
  red, pickled, 128, 129
oranges:
  cake, 132
  crêpes with strawberry sauce, 37
  and roast pork salad, 72
  sliced, with cinnamon, 40
organization, 155–156

Packaging, 155
pancakes:
  baked puffed, 121
  corn, 121
  potato, 64
  whole wheat, 120–121
panfried trout with bacon, 61
pans, 157
parslied chick-pea dip, 101
pasta:
  angel hair, with asparagus and smoked salmon, 137
  fusilli with peanut sauce, 73
  with ham and eggs, 136
  thin, with chopped fresh tomato sauce, 137
pastitsio, 145
pâté, Dorothy's chicken liver, 89
pea and rice salad, 25
peanut butter cookies, 133
peanut sauces, 73, 96
pears and apples, sautéed, with hard sauce, 45
pecans:
  carrot bread, 68–69
  moons, 21
  smoked chicken salad with dates and, 129
peppers, bell:
  ham and potato frittata, 68
  linguiça with, 53
  roasted, artichoke hearts and, 81
  roasted red, 84
peppers, chile, 13, 141
pickled dishes:
  fish, old-fashioned, 89
  red onion and beef salad, 128
  red onions, 128, 129
  shrimp, 101